Salvaging Capitalism

Saving Democracy

How wealth extraction, stock market games, and politics are stealing our future.

Dr. Bob Abell

ISBN-13: 978-1480081215
ISBN-10: 1480081213

Dedication

This book is dedicated to the generations that have gone before, and the seven plus generations that will (hopefully) follow, and make the world a better place.

It is dedicated to my departed parents, to a mother who was kind and gentle, loved people, animals, birds, and flowers, and had the patience of Job. And to a father who was driven, through tragedy at an early age, to make life better for himself and his family, who understood honest hard work, and believed fervently that we needed the education that had been denied him through circumstance.

It is dedicated to my children, from whom I have learned many things, and who have contributed to my growth, to my business as critics, partners, and trusted employees, and to my future as a father and grandfather. And it is their future, and their children's future, both the promise and the peril, which is at stake here.

And finally, first to my wife of 42 years, my soul-mate, business partner, lover, professional editor, dance partner, and fiercest and most relentless critic. Her passion for humanity, her spirituality, unabashed love for and interest in all cultures, all peoples, and all the wonders of creation, have helped to guide and sustain me throughout my life, and throughout this intense and difficult birthing of ideas on paper.

Acknowledgement

I also wish to acknowledge the members of the local chapter of The Alternative Board: Chip, David, Greg, Tim, Moodie, and Doug, for sharing their stories, business acumen, and what was "under the kimono" as their companies underwent growth, acquisition, mergers, ownership changes, personnel issues, contract issues, marketing issues, and all of the panoply of life in the corporation in this decade.

Our over three years of regular monthly meetings to – in confidence – discuss shared problems, to critically appraise actions and directions, strategies and tactics, financing and labor relations, and to try to provide advice, questions to ponder, and a time to reflect, was surely an opportunity greater than any Ivy League school could possibly provide to study entrepreneurship close up, and to better understand how parts of the business world otherwise hidden to me in my small corner of that world really operate.

Thanks to the following for reading an early draft and providing valuable feedback: Evelyn Abell, Kendrick Abell, Tony Broomfield, Erwin Dreessen, Cliff and Bev Floyd, Dr. John Jeffery, Howard Sommerfeld.

Editor: Evelyn A. Abell

Forward

This book is written for all of you who consider yourself part of the middle class, and also for those who once were or should have been, or should now by hard work, by education and/or by experience be in the middle class in North America, but are not!

We are currently facing the greatest transfer of wealth out of the hands of the middle class to ever occur in history, and over a comparatively short period. I pondered the implications of that for myself, for my children, for my grandchildren, and I did not like the picture that emerged. This book is my attempt to share that picture, and to suggest ways to change it.

If you already know a lot about capital and how it plays out in the stock market, and how that in turn affects whether you or your children have a decent job, or any job at all, then there are parts of this narrative you might breeze through and say "Yes of course, I knew that already." Other parts might come as a real surprise.

As a businessman, and very small player in the stock market, I thought I knew quite a bit as well, but the more research I did, the more concerned I became that our whole North American economy is broken – and not by accident.

But there are **hundreds of millions** in North America who leave all of this to their broker, or their mutual fund manager, or for the vast majority, to their pension funds administrator. And you assume that the financial institutions and the government are watching out for your interests. If you are one of those people, is it important for you to understand what has actually happened? You betcha.

Perhaps doubly important, since you are the big majority, and you buy products, and you vote in elections, and when companies and politicians screw up, you pay the price. Am I suggesting you take over handling your own stocks or pensions? Absolutely not! But you do owe it to yourself and to your children to know what is going on.

So I have quite deliberately erred on the side of explaining some things that many might already know, with apologies to people like my economist friend who asked me, "Do you think people have been living under a rock for the last thirty years?"

To which my answer is "no". Rather it is like the "boiling frog" story. The changes have been very slow, "raising the temperature" only a fraction of a degree at a time. And often the really bad actors have hidden their behavior or their motives; have both seduced and "snowed" us.

The problems are massive and systemic, and far from transparent. If the system is going to be fixed, if it can be fixed at this late stage, we cannot assume that big business and government will fix it of their own accord.

They, acting together, got us into this mess. It happened slowly, over about forty years, but the negative effects have greatly accelerated since 2000.

This book is my attempt to make some sense out of what has happened to our economy, our personal savings, and our dreams for the future – and why. It is an attempt to explain the issues in simple terms that you, I, and other outsiders (as opposed to insiders) can understand. And finally, it is an attempt to offer some suggestions of where things went off the rails, and how we, both individually and collectively, can help get them back on track.

Even now, our own governments – pushed hard by multinational businesses and foreign governments – are making decisions daily that are not in your or my best long-term interests. We need to individually and collectively push back, and reverse direction, while there is still time.

Contents

"But hang it, Jim, you've clean missed the point—blame it, you've missed it a thousand mile."

"Who? Me? Go 'long. Doan' talk to me 'bout yo' pints. I reck'n I knows sense when I sees it; en dey ain' no sense in sich doin's as dat. ... Doan' talk to me 'bout Sollermun, Huck, I knows him by de back."

"But I tell you, you don't get the point."

"Blame de point! I reck'n I knows what I knows.

(Mark Twain, The Adventures of Huckleberry Finn, 1884)

Chapter 1 – Literary Devices, Confessions, and Superheros

The problems are complex. Most of us, like Mark Twain's Jim, "knows what we knows". But Jim was pretty much on the mark with most of his judgments of character, recognizing scoundrels as scoundrels (if just a spot confused on the subject of Solomon). Jim was much less likely than Huck to "follow the party line", and a more astute judge of character than many of us seem to be today.

The South in Huck's time was a complex and systematically-unfair social structure, and changing that structure put the U.S. though some of the toughest and bloodiest times in its history. That makes a good metaphor for where we are today, and if you have not read Huck Finn, or think it's a kid's book, dig into it some lazy sunny afternoon. Professor Ben Click describes it as follows:

> "Twain's novel is universally considered ... 'fine and noble, and enduring' – and yet it is also one of the most banned books of all time. Currently, it ranks #14 in the Top 100 Banned or Challenged Books of the last decade. In the decade preceding that, it ranked #5....
>
> (Ben Click, Professor of English, St. Mary's College of Maryland, www.betterlivingthroughbeowulf.com/?p=6616)

Banned multiple times through history for multiple reasons –
because some people "clean missed the point", both the inherent
truth in Twain's characterization of the injustice of the society of
the day, and the importance of his choice of idiom and language in
the telling.

And because it might "corrupt youth" in telling the story of one
brave and conflicted young boy who decided he would break the
laws of the land, and possibly his shot at the Pearly Gates, because
he genuinely cared for another human being, and came in time to
understand that the laws were unjust.

In the twenty-first century, mankind is facing some similarly
complex and unfair structures, and to fix the structural problems is
going to be very tough. The solutions require huge changes in the
ways we act, in the ways we think, and in the ways we
communicate to those who are a part of the solution, and those
who are a part of the problem. And as a society, we need to
enforce some laws and change others.

Faced with the reality of what has gone on, it would be easy to
become confused, depressed, and sad, and to therefore feel
helpless.

So I will use some literary devices, and some tools, terms, and
techniques from the worlds of continuous improvement and
systems theory – difficult terms like "sticky notes", and "box",
and "root cause", and "waste"; that kind of tough stuff. The sticky
notes are grist for the team meeting, so I will also prepare "my
notes for the team meeting". Bring yours along too.

And, with apologies in advance to Dr. Seuss:

> But this topic is messy, so big and so tall,
> That it could become hard to read it at all.
> So in with the prickles, we'll sprinkle some smiles,
> Call the crooks "tapeworms", and dump on their styles.

To accomplish this, we will use some "folksy language", "The Box Game", "Bimbo monologues", "Worm monologues", and "Cheerleader awards" to try to break down hundreds of years of slavish adoration of certain people simply because they *have money*, regardless of how many lives they destroyed in obtaining it – the slavish adoration that allows, even encourages them to keep us enslaved.

Some of these people are truly a joke, a "jest of the gods". Time we up the ante. The monologues are what we should be saying to these people, if we were not so polite. We have very recent video and audio evidence that in their private sanctums, when they think they are "off-mike", they say worse things about the rest of us, and laugh or smirk, or "wink, wink, nod, nod".

So I will be impolite to types of people who truly are a bad joke on humanity, on behalf of all of the polite folks out there who are not ready to do so. We need to laugh at these people, not envy or adore them.

In addition to a slavish adoration of moneyed folks, we also keep quite a number of "sacred cows" in the pasture. These strongly held beliefs get seriously in the way of rational dialog. But killing sacred cows sounds too unpleasant, so I have settled on another metaphor. Did you ever comment that you have to "walk on eggs" around some folks, or around some topics in certain company? So have I. So we will need to crack some eggs!

Confessions

It would not be possible to capture the full scale of either the problems or the solutions in one small book, even if I knew and fully understood everything that has happened in history, could foretell the future with pinpoint accuracy, and had the combined power of a military division of cosmic super-heroes.

Most of us don't have super brains, and have not been bitten by a radioactive spider or irradiated with kryptonite. But we all know what we know, can influence what we can influence, and can do what we as individuals and working together in teams can do. We also, at least for a short time in history, have access to real information, in real depth, in real time.

So that is going to have to substitute for the Wisdom of Solomon. If, as happened to Huck, we gradually begin to see problems in the way the world turns, we have access to fact-check quickly and in depth. So we need to go from *"I knows what I knows"* to *"I knows how to find out"*.

So you understand where I am coming from, I will 'fess up. I am **not an expert** on stocks and securities, or on politics, or on the law, or on economic theory, or finance, or on any number of the specialties that revolve around these "mysterious" worlds, but I do "… know how to find out".

I am trained in science as a chemist, then in education as a teacher. I am also a student of history, with a special interest in the rise and fall of empires – the builders and destroyers, the enlightened and the despots.

In graduate studies I was exposed to an esoteric mix of psychology, statistics, computing, and systems theory. After an eight-year stint in academia, I became an entrepreneur in 1981, founding a business with a prime focus on technology-based training. Business process improvement is currently our primary focus.

Salvaging Capitalism?

I was driven to undertake this book by a fractious and at times farcical U.S. Presidential Election campaign, an unprecedented assault on the environment by the current government in Ottawa, and finally by a LinkedIn discussion group which asked the deliberately provocative question:

> "Why would global communism not be a
> viable means to ecological sustainability?"

Having grown up in an age when U.S. domestic and foreign policy seemed largely driven by a concern that there was a communist under every bed, I have been conditioned to see and also to understand that communism is not a good thing. And I haven't really changed my mind on that!

But at the same time, like Hamlet, I have a sense that "Something is rotten in the state of Denmark". At a time when we should be advancing in overall happiness and well being in Western democracies and around the world – with the "evil empire" of the Marxist/Leninist/Stalinist crew vanquished – we seem instead to be losing ground, and sinking into the abyss. Capitalism is failing us at a critical juncture in history.

Some think Capitalism cannot be salvaged. Some think Capitalism should not be saved! I had a post from one such person recently. I understand this attitude, and sympathize with this attitude. Yes, we need entirely new models, and sustainable models, and fair and equitable models, and science driven models – which will take time to build, to nurture, and to define.

So I have a vision of the future - but also a pragmatism that leads me to think we must move incrementally. We can't swim well enough to deliberately sink the Capitalist Ark we are sailing in, even if it is beyond salvaging.

As I see it, we have four choices:
- Jump overboard and try to swim away before it sucks us down, although the nearest shore is a thousand miles away;
- Bail like hell and ignore the holes in the side as irrelevant;
- Close our eyes, strike up the band, and go down with the ship; or
- Patch as many of the holes as we can and try to limp to port.

We can't wait for the Superheroes to save the day!

Saving Democracy?

I originally had the subtitle: "The 5S's of "securities": how they are destroying our country, our wealth, and our freedom – and what we need to do about it." But the more research I did, the more convinced I became that the financial problems that have been foisted on us are indeed a clear and present danger to democracy itself. Extreme? Alarmist? You be the judge. I sincerely hope I am wrong. Perhaps you can find the flaws in my thinking.

Ideally, both my ideas and your ideas will be taken forward and actually discussed and acted upon in real circles of influence, and real changes will result. These changes will ultimately play out in ways that are sure to differ from the initial vision I am sketching here.

It will take expert teams of dedicated people who really care about positive results for all, to move us forward as positive /enlightened/ honest/real/ interconnected dreamers envision. It is not "my idea" but "our idea", where collectively all of us engaging together generate better results than any of us possibly could alone.

And it will take all of us, pulling in more or less the same general direction. It will involve harnessing the boundless idealism and sense of justice that characterizes most young people, when they come face to face with reality and choices – as Huck did.

"The Middle Class has been buried ..."
(Mitt Romney, 1ˢᵗ Presidential Debate, 2012)

Chapter 2 – R.I.P. Middle Class

There have been tremendous advances in manufacturing productivity using a process improvement methodology called Lean Manufacturing. It is based on the very simple concept that every process in manufacturing should add value for the customer, and any process that does not add value is waste. This applies equally to service industries from merchandizing to health care.

Would the application of these principles and methods to government and to the financial underpinnings of the Capitalist system of wealth generation yield comparable improvements in value for the "customers" of these systems and organizations?

Given the loads of manure that emanate from politicians and parties, and the massive destruction of the economy by irresponsible financial institutions, it would seem difficult to imagine that there is not room for huge improvements in "customer" and "shareholder" value – and we are all both shareholders and customers in this economy in one way or another. We all have skin in the game and chips on the table.

But if you have been a representative member of the predominant middle class in America, your stock of chips has been disappearing at an alarming rate. According to the Federal Reserve, the middle class in the U.S. bore the brunt of a "wealth decline" of 39% between 2007 and 2010 – bringing that group back in absolute dollar terms to about where they were in 1992, without adjusting for inflation. One reporter headed the story "R.I.P. Middle Class".

At the same time, a recent estimate suggests that $19 Trillion is controlled by just 0.001 percent of the World's population. That is some $3 Trillion greater than the current (and rising) debt of the entire US treasury. The inequity is up sharply. How did this happen?

The media on both left and right likes to talk about "the destruction of wealth". A recent Google search on the explicit term string "wealth destruction" generated 138,000 hits. I believe that this use of terminology is deliberately misleading.

It makes it sound as if somebody has made or intends to make a huge bonfire of thousand-dollar bills, and set it aflame. This is, of course, bull-twiddle. No one is actually destroying money. If you had money, and you don't have it now, someone else does.

Even if a currency is devalued, that simply means that all holders of that currency have decreased buying power, and all holders of other currencies have a comparative increase in buying power, so there has been a de facto transfer of money.

Since the 2012 U.S. election, this media narrative has largely addressed right wing concerns, the wealth of the wealthy, whereas prior to the election much of the narrative concerned main street Americans, who individually and collectively wondered how their wealth had been so quickly "destroyed".

Wealth was not destroyed. Though a whole series of complex transactions, substantial amounts of money were ultimately transferred from your bank account, and your assets, and your pension funds, and even from your government, directly or indirectly into the hands of the super rich around the World, which made them even more "super rich".

The words we use to describe things have powerful effects on our response to events. Consider that you are on vacation, and a neighbor calls. He delivers one of the following three messages of catastrophe.

"John, I hate to be the bearer of bad news, but:
1) your house burned down last night."
2) some broker just sold your house, and the new owners are moving in on Tuesday."
3) house movers arrived, jacked your house off the foundation and took it away."

Will your response be the same? No? Then perhaps it is important to recognize the difference between "wealth destruction", "fraud", and outright "theft".

Is it Out of Our Control or Beyond Our Control?

The easiest way to dis-empower one's self is to believe that we cannot effect change or influence change. Or to believe that things are beyond our control, and we have to just accept that this is the way the world works. So a large part of the machine that is responsible for this massive transfer of wealth spends a significant amount of money and effort to convince us we are helpless.

They accomplish this by a combination of smoke screens and disinformation that would make the members of "The Party" in Orwell's 1984 beam with pride.

Let me be clear before going on, that many people – through specialist training and/or a self-selecting and self-limiting perspective – might inadvertently get sucked into this game without realizing they are being used. Alternately, they might be fully aware, and expect to be rewarded for their efforts, either through financial gain or through the "approval" of the "big guns". By omission or commission, they become the cheerleaders for the system.

It would be a life's work in itself to try to figure out which "expert" is hoping for approval or financial gain and which "expert" is just getting sucked in, and frankly is not worth the effort. But it is important to be "suspicious" and to keep the "bullshit detector" set to maximum sensitivity. It is far more important to pay attention to what is on the shovel, than to who is holding it.

So What Gives?

Economist Thomas F. Cooley published an article in Forbes.com in 2009 titled: "Has Rising Inequity Destroyed the Middle Class?" In that article he noted that the share of income earned by the top 10% dropped from a peak of nearly 50% prior to the Great Depression to around 35% in the post WWII period. But after about 1982, the share of the top 10% "took off". By 2006, it was back close to the 50%. He went on to observe that most of the "action" was in the top 1%.

Warren Buffett explained it this way: "There's class warfare, all right, but it's my class, the rich class, that's making war, and we're winning."

(I should mention, lest you get the wrong idea, that Buffet clearly does not think this is a good thing.)

But according to Cooley, technological change is the "most compelling argument" for this huge shift in income distribution. He then calls for higher levels of educational investment and innovation.

Cooley's attribution of cause seems a most curious statement, more akin to a party line suitable for publication by Forbes than to a clearheaded analysis of the facts. Having neatly sidestepped any political issues, or any capital issues, he puts it all down to an **obvious** effect of technology.

That, of course, dis-empowers us! Technology is here to stay. Who can argue against innovation? Education is a good thing, right?

This shows the danger in using the wrong measures for any analysis of a complex situation. Cooley makes the case that labor's share of output has remained essentially constant for over 50 years. I can't dispute his facts on this particular measure. But his choice of "labor's share of output" as an appropriate metric could be seen as a bit of "slight of hand" guaranteed to disadvantage labor in his argument.

In fact, his numbers seem at considerable variance with those of Les Leopold in his insightful book: <u>The Looting of America: How Wall Street's Game of Fantasy Finance Destroyed Our Jobs, Pensions, and Prosperity, and What We Can Do About It.</u>

In fact, labor cost as a percentage of the total cost of production has been decreasing ever since the invention of waterpower and the steam engine. Labor productivity in the U.S. is remarkably high compared to many other countries, and access to technology is widespread. Yet many economies have drastically outperformed the U.S. throughout the past decade.

Leopold graphically displays the sudden divergence of the productivity vs. labor-wage graph, beginning around 1973. Although Leopold does not dwell on the historical aspects, it is important to realize this occurred at a time when there was a recession in Europe, the Yon Kippur War, OPEC retaliation, the surge in Japanese car sales in the U.S., extrication from Vietnam, and Nixon's initiatives in China – followed shortly by Sam Walton's visits to Asia in 1975 – the start of Wal-Mart's love affair with (Communist) China that would so impact American manufacturing over the next 30 years.

In point of fact, as Leopold points out, productivity continued to climb from then until the present era, but wages – adjusted for inflation – stagnated for over 30 years. One consequence of this wage stagnation was ever-increasing debt for the middle class.

And if, as Cooley maintains, "…labor's share of output has remained remarkably constant at roughly 70% from 1950 through 2008", how does that jive with the bill of goods sold to shareholders that the only way to stay competitive in a global economy is to outsource labor jobs to low wage countries? Increasing labor costs have been the whipping boy for CEOs for the last 30 years. Tilt!

Other analysts have picked up on this as well. Steve Minter, writing on-line in Industry Week, asks the question: "Did American Capitalism Take a Wrong Turn?" He quotes Pulitzer

Prize-winning journalist Hedrick Smith, author of "Who Stole the American Dream?"

> "Over the years, Smith says, there has been a growing divergence between the fortunes of business and of the middle class. From 1948-1973, productivity in the U.S. rose 96.8% while the hourly compensation for workers went up 93.7%. But since 1973, productivity has risen 80% and hourly compensation has increased just 10%."

That Cooley might have picked the wrong measures is not a new game. The statement widely attributed to Disraeli (among others) that: "There are three kinds of lies: lies, damned lies, and statistics", perhaps sums up the problem in a nutshell.

Of course anyone who has had the fortune (or misfortune) to actually study statistics, knows that statistics do not allow you to directly attribute causality, in spite of the fact that we do it all the time. Nor do they allow us to reliably propose solutions.

But let's follow Cooley's argument and his proposed solution for just one moment. What we need, according to Cooley, is higher levels of educational investment and innovation. Yet the crash of 1929 came at a time when innovation was raging. New cars, airplanes, improved communications, better schools, Ford's industrial innovations, everything seemed it was "Smashing! Just smashing!" to quote Thoroughly Modern Millie. Then in 1929, it all came crashing down. Did the technology fall apart? Was the educated class suddenly rendered stupid? Seems unlikely to me.

Fast forward to the 1990's. The Internet is alive and well, technology is roaring. Technology companies are leading the pack. Furthermore, the technological revolution is spilling into other industries, increasing visibility of operations, opening up new marketing avenues, and generally spreading the wealth around. Do you think decreased innovation was the culprit in the 2001 tech crash, or as some would call it, the "bear market correction"? How about 2008?

Ah, but what was happening in education? Maybe Cooley missed the mark on wages and technology but was right about the education deficit. Surely there must have been a problem there.

Well, according to the Association of Universities and Colleges of Canada, things there were "smashing, just smashing" too. Though the 1990's, full-time enrollment climbed from roughly 450 thousand in 1990 to 550 thousand by 2000. By 2010, it was over 750,000. Now based on the similar demographics between the U.S. and Canada, and also noting the number of unemployed university graduates that have showed up with placards on Wall Street, it is somewhat difficult to give much credence to Cooley's explanation for, or solution to the problem. So ….

The Cheerleader Award – goes to (drum roll) - Thomas F. Cooley!

[**Caution:** This is our first presentation of this coveted award, so I will remind you just this one time that specialist training and/or self-selecting and self-limiting perspectives might inadvertently cause really "good" folks to get sucked into cheerleading for the games, without actually realizing they are being used. Many truly believe this is the way the world works. And maybe they are right and I'm wrong. Alternately, they might be fully aware. Like any court, in the court of public opinion we need to consider most "Cheerleaders" innocent, unless sufficient evidence piles up to prove collusion beyond the shadow of a doubt.]

So if it is not really technology, and it is not really education, something else is going on here. And that something is leading us like sheep to the slaughter – back to the glory days of feudalism and serfdom, and Divine Kings. In a wacko world of sound bites and instant gratification, in a world where product placement game shows and phony reality shows capture far more attention than real news and situational analysis, we are on the cusp of the fall of the 2nd "Roman Empire". The barbarians are at the gates, but dressed in Armani suits, sporting Rolex watches, and trophy brides. (Did I mention hairpieces?)

Sorry, let me re-phase that. The barbarians are already inside the gates! Some came in a Trojan horse labeled "Safety and Security", preceded by a vast array of hangers-on blowing smoke screens from multiple orifices. Others arrived shouting "jobs, jobs!" without mentioning that either these jobs would be at a near-slave wage, or else overseas – where slaves are cheaper and generally more compliant – or the jobs would be dependent on an agreement to total destruction of the environment and sacrifice of the future of our children and all of humanity.

The problem, in a nutshell, is that the role of capital in our capitalist society has been completely and utterly perverted. How did that happen? Leopold describes the problem through a long-term financial lens, which elevated "money from money" as the new path to prosperity, replacing the notion of "money from production".

This is a long-term "**strategic**" view, and a perfectly valid and necessary way to look at the problem. This problem has to be addressed. This is a war we have to win.

In this book, I focus in on the up close and personal "**tactics**", the short-term processes and violent disruptions that attend this strategy, though the application of the 5Ss of the "Securities Game". These are battles we have to win.

The rich have always liked their games. Staples of the old world include croquet, riding to hounds, and gambling. In America, it is golf, tennis, and gun sports, and of course gambling. For those who can't afford the equipment or the membership fees, there are, of course spectator sports – baseball, basketball, soccer, and hockey. The rich participate in these as well, as owners and promoters. (And players.)

There is nothing seriously wrong with this picture, until the games start to have a negative affect on society. There are two primary ways this can happen. One is that games become distractions that obscure other genuine concerns. This was first recognized as an effective political tool by the Roman Senate around 123 B.C.E. and was denounced by the Roman satirist Juvenal, who stated:

"… Already long ago, from when we sold our vote
to no man, the People have abdicated our duties;
for the People who once upon a time handed out
military command, high civil office, legions –
everything, now restrains itself and anxiously
hopes for just two things: **bread and circuses."**

Having watched the anxiousness and the huge volume of press
coverage that attends any contract talks threatening delay of the
new football, hockey, or baseball season, I think we have moved a
long way down that path – a path that in Rome led to collapse of
the Republic, rule by autocratic emperors, ultimately to the fall of
the empire – and 500 years of chaos referred to as the Dark Ages.

The second primary way that games have a negative effect is
when games become the alternative to real life, and "games" in
the business world become a serious hazard to our health and
well-being. Are people playing games with the lifeblood of North
American commerce? Most assuredly!

Now I have unabashedly appropriated the term "5S" from the
Lean Manufacturing world. In that world, it is used to describe a
waste removal process involving 5 steps, all beginning with the
letter "S" – usually rendered as: Sort, Set-in-order, Shine,
Standardize, and Sustain – a part of a systematic effort to improve
business processes and competitiveness.

But in the 5S "Securities Game", it is a *waste generating process*,
deliberately designed to remove value from the system – to
transfer that value from your pocket into someone else's pocket
without your being able to prevent it. The 5Ss of the "securities
game" are: the Shill Game; the Shell Game; the Short Game; the
Steal Game; and the Secured-Creditors Game.

For the insiders, it is all just a game – a competitive game in
which they win and you lose. For some it is not even about the
money. After a certain point, the money has no meaning - unless
you want to roll in it like Scrooge McDuck. It is about power,
about feeling "superior". It is about being on the Forbes Real-

Times Billionaires site. Just gotta know who made $292.71 Million in the market today!

But if you are an outsider, it is the health and well being of your family, and your rights to life, liberty, and the pursuit of happiness that these "high-rollers" are playing with. The very existence of the Forbes "Real-Time Billionaires" website is an affront to every middle and upper-middle class working person in America. The Billionaire's version of the Reality Show. So ...

The next Cheerleader Award – goes to (drum roll) – "Forbes.com", for showing us that keeping up with the Billionaire Jones is what makes the world turn!

Organization of This Book

This book is roughly organized around three big themes.

First, chapters 3 through 7 attempt to examine and explain the growth of Capitalism as a system – with all of its splendor and its warts, and its reliance on that funny stuff called "money".

Most of what has happened in the last forty years had happened before; and had been acted on by governments, discussed by philosophers, and modified to make a workable system.

Many of the Cheerleaders for what is currently going down misconstrue this history, and misquote or misrepresent the persons and ideas that arose in the historical context. I learned a ton of interesting things doing this research. I hope you find it as interesting and helpful to you as it was to me. I have deliberately left room throughout to allow you to note down your ideas on all of this. This is a team effort.

Chapters 8 though 13 deal with the stock market, and the stock market games that have been directly responsible for many of the short-term problems that have cost jobs, resulted in under-funded pension plans, government bailouts, and "fiscal cliffs".

Each of the "Game" chapters concludes with my take on what constitutes the root problems, and what actions we might want to take to fix them. Many of the fixes could happen quickly, if we had the political will.

And finally, chapters 14 though 17 look at problems in government, in the relationship between government and corporations, and between government and the public that they presumably represent. All of that needs fixing, and the timelines are short.

It is a strategic battle that either will be won by an informed and involved public, or will be won by those who don't honor democracy and don't believe in freedom and equality, issuing in a world that I don't want to be a part of, nor wish for my children and grandchildren.

Notes:

_____

_____

_____

_____

_____

_____

_____

_____

_____

_____

"Capital is money, capital is commodities. By virtue of it being value, it has acquired the occult ability to add value to itself. It brings forth living offspring, or, at the least, lays golden eggs."
(Karl Marx "Das Kapital" {Capital: A Critique of Political Economy} 1867)

Chapter 3 – The Capital in "Capitalism"

So what is Capitalism anyway, can it be salvaged, and why is it worth saving? Are there alternatives? Is there only one flavor and color of Capitalism, and is it always licorice?

There is a tendency in political circles to deliberately obscure the obvious, so capitalism and communism have tended to get all muddled up with political systems of democracy and freedom vs. totalitarianism and absolute rule. Capitalism is an economic system, not a political system.

The recipe is pretty simple. In order to create something, it takes two ingredients – money, and effort – also called Capital and Labor. The Capital supplies both the equipment and raw materials, and the labor then uses that equipment to transform the raw materials and create something new – something with more value than the starting materials. Without these two ingredients, Capital and Labor, you can't even make even a cake – literally!

But of course money is just an exchange medium we use to buy stuff, stuff that somebody else created with his or her labor, so it all comes down ultimately to effort and to labor. Money, or Capital, is just a catalyst for moving the labor assets around to make stuff, and make stuff happen.

Scotsman Adam Smith, a firm believer in Capitalism, made this pretty clear, devoting to "money" an entire chapter of his economic treatise: <u>An Inquiry Into the Nature and Causes of the Wealth of Nations</u>, first released coincidently in 1776 – an otherwise important date in North America. But we tend to forget what money really is at times – with serious consequences.

Marx described Capitalists as "controlling the means of production", by which he simply meant that Capitalists owned the factories that employed the people that made stuff. This created a much better system than what it replaced, which was largely a combination of hand labor, and forms of organized theft called feudalism, colonialism, and mercantilism.

So Capitalists were people who had money, and could use this Capital to make stuff, and make stuff happen. Pretty simple really.

Where did these Capitalists come from? Was it some freak of birth? Well yes, pretty much. It really helps one to become a Capitalist if one has "old money". In fact, for a long time in society, "new money" and the people that had it – "les nouveaux riches" – were frowned upon as somehow inferior.

That had the unfortunate effect of making some of the "new money" people even more pretentious and obnoxious than the "old money" people, and to an incredible extent plays out in what is going on today.

Notes:

_____

_____

_____

_____

_____

_____

_____

_____

"Fathers shall not be put to death because of their children, nor shall children be put to death because of their fathers. Each one shall be put to death for his own sin. Deuteronomy 24:16

Chapter 4 – Old Money and New Money – A Side Note

Now the following is a bit of an aside, but sort of an interesting aside. It has some hints, however, at how things work. It also would help the discussion going forward if some of the Capitalists of today got down off their high horse, put their gun back in the holster, and said "Yup, that were my pappy a'right!"

So let's look at "old money". Old money is not a description of moldy bills piled up in a heap somewhere. Old money is money that has "been in the family" for time immemorial. So where did it come from in the first place? Well that's pretty much why it's immemorial, or not in memory – deliberately.

There is a certain inconvenient truth that most if not all "old money" came from practices now largely if not completely officially frowned upon. If you were born with a silver spoon in your mouth, your pappy, or his pappy, or his pappy's pappy might have had some answering to do at the Pearly Gates.

One of the first and foremost sources of old money was outright theft though raids, wars, and piracy, which took money, land, or resources that did not belong to the perpetrator. The Spaniards, the French, the Portuguese, and the English were all very good at this. But so were the Romans, the Egyptians, the Mongols, the Aztec – and many aboriginal groups when the going got tough. Later in history, they were joined by the Belgians, the Germans, the Russians, and Japanese. And the Church – don't forget the Church! Pick your flavor. They all did it. It is in the history books. So did the U.S. – yes, really!

Then there was Usury – the loaning of money and collection of interest on same. Because of certain religious practice that banned this – presumably because of a nasty scene in a temple in

Jerusalem about two millennia ago – the supply of money was restricted for a long period of history, which made an extremely profitable business for those not so constrained.

At the same time, it made the moneylenders subject to serious problems when their debtors decided it was easier to beat them up or even kill them rather than pay the debt. So lots of old money can be traced to this artificial restriction of the money supply for presumed religious reasons. Lots of other problems that continue to bedevil the world to this very day were a more or less direct side effect of the beating and killing.

Then there was the semi-legalized theft called "privateering", in which party A licensed party B to be a pirate, as long as he promised to steal only from the "enemy", party C. Follow old money in Canada, and it often traces back to privateering – much of it instigated by the British against their sworn enemy, the upstart breakaway American States.

What really **old** money in Canada does not come from privateering comes from land grants – generally to military people including our Canadian "Loyalists", thrown out of the new United States as "Traitors". Now the fact that much of the land involved in these "grants" was inconveniently occupied by earlier peoples was unfortunate – at least for the earlier inhabitants – but then they simply seemed quite incapable of running to the local land registry to show they really "owned" it.

And of course when the some 60,000 "Traitors" were thrown out of the new United States, their assets – land, property, slaves, and money – were forfeit to Patriots, which created new "old money" as well.

Now my Great-Great-Great-Grandpappy, if my genealogy is correct, was involved in the land grant business in P.E.I. in the 1700s. If he and his wife had not been such total scumbags, I might have old money too! But as it happened, he was run through with a bayonet by an Irish tenant farmer, who from all accounts did the rest of the world a favor. Oh well!

And finally, there was slavery. Of all the thefts that occurred through history, this was the worst, and is an ancient practice, recounted in the Bible (which was then of course used to justify the practice for centuries). The theft of a man's freedom has to rank above all other violations of property.

It would be nice to think that chapter of history is long dead, but of course it is not. Forced labor, child labor, forced prostitution – these all exist today. Many North American people – and many multinational corporations – tend to turn a blind eye. And as a result, it just might be getting worse again, rather than better.

New Money

Funny how making things hard to get ultimately creates fortunes. Usury in the middle ages, rum in the twenties, and drugs today. If much early old money in Canada came from privateering, it pales in comparison to the money that later flowed in from south of our border when the Yanks bought into prohibition. Of course it made a lot of money in the U.S. too, and the criminal subclass of nouveau riche that resulted had – and continue to have – a large influence in how things work in the U.S. today.

There was a recent scandal about the influence of Columbian drug-money laundering in the U.S. and connections of Columbian Drug family members with certain Capital companies that did a lot of outsourcing of American jobs.

Then some paparazzi got a long distance photo shot of some Royal skin, and the drugs and money scandal quickly vanished from the front page. "Plus ça change, plus c'est la même chose."

Notes:

"... They built the mines, mills and the factories, for the good of us all"
(Gordon Lightfoot, "The Great Canadian Railroad Trilology")

Chapter 5 – Capitalism and the Building of America

So in the early days of a prosperous and growing America, the "Yup, that were my pappy alright!" guys had the money, and many of them started doing useful things with it. Many of them did so in communities where they lived, building the mines, mills, and factories. This ushered in a new age of prosperity for millions, much as Adam Smith had foreseen. The U.S. became a very wealthy nation.

In feudal times, the only way you could make real money was by owning land. That was pretty much the choice. If you were not a landowner, you were a serf or a slave, with no say in how things were run, and no security. The only way out was military service – which also largely served to make things better for landowners and mercantilists.

With the growth of industry, all of a sudden you could work for a wage! And you had choices of employer! Things were looking up. You could vote without being a landowner. Soon you could even vote if you were born female. What an innovation!

The old world "Barons" – feudal landowners – were replaced by the new "Barons of Industry". Interesting how the term survived.

When Adam Smith wrote his famous economy treatise, the term capitalism was not yet in use. Smith talks about a "system of perfect liberty" or "system of natural liberty". A system of perfect liberty! Now who would not cheer for our side?

Of course in 1776, he made a few assumptions about how the world works, and what could and could not be done to mess up your "perfect liberty". These assumptions were based on the laws, processes, and technology of the time. There was no New York Stock Exchange. There were no labor unions. There was no Fed. Bank lending practices were still severely restricted.

And there was this really effective system called the "free market", in which all things naturally balance themselves out, guided by the "invisible hand" of competition. This made the intercession of government in the process largely ineffective and totally unwelcome. Government inevitably made matters worse. So thought Adam Smith in 1776 – as do Libertarians in 2012.

But Smith himself did see some "gotcha's" in all of this, and made some pretty strong statements about certain behaviors that should not occur. He was, after all, not just an economist, but also a moral philosopher, having earlier written his Theory of Moral Sentiments, in which he explained the natural interplay of propriety, prudence, and benevolence, self-love, reason, and sentiment. Do you find it strange that most of these topics don't make prime time in the business schools, business magazines, or business TV nowadays?

A later philosopher and economist took up some of the same themes in his writings in the late 1800's. By this time there actually was a New York Stock Exchange, but no real labor unions, and no Fed, as yet. There was a revolution going on – an industrial revolution. The philosopher and economist was Karl Marx, and his work quickly made him the man all Capitalists are taught to hate from a very young age.

This largely discourages any discussion of his theories, which, like those of Adam Smith, were forged in a different age. Where he really diverged from Smith was in Smith's implicit assumptions about the role of the market, and particularly about the "invisible hand" and the moral sentiments that were part and parcel of Smith's worldview.

Marx considered that society represented an ongoing struggle between an ownership class, the capitalists, and a working class of labor, the proletariat, and that the church was heavily involved in maintaining the status quo.

Marx got a lot of stuff wrong. He thought that social revolution would first occur in the highly industrialized and somewhat democratic countries like Germany and England. Instead it occurred in agrarian Czarist Russia. He thought that socialist governments would eventually give way to a Utopia of class-less-ness called communism. He thought this was inevitable. Instead, the reality of communism led to nothing even vaguely like a Utopia, before collapsing in disarray near the end of the 20th century.

Early American Capitalists paid no attention to Marx's musings. They kept building and expanding, and innovating as they did so, with lumber mills, and textiles, shipyards, and auto plants. Henry Ford introduced the moving assembly line starting around 1908, and worker specialization that made vehicles much cheaper – an affordable commodity.

Ford even increased pay for his own workers substantially above the competition, and brought in programs of "benefits" for his workers. He had this novel idea that his employees should make enough to buy the products they were building. American productivity and innovation soared.

The Labor Movement

But not all Capitalists had the vision of Henry Ford, and not all was roses in this rush to industrialization. Some of the squalid factory conditions that Charles Dickens so vividly described in his novels set in the mid to late 1800's in England (coincidentally then home to Karl Marx) emerged in the U.S. as well.

Laurence, Massachusetts, situated on the Merrimac River, had capitalized on the abundant waterpower and large immigrant population to build a textile industry, which by 1912 employed some 32,000 men, women, and children.

But as increased mechanization enabled higher productivity, owners cut the workforce dramatically. And having thereby reduced the labor demand, they were able to drastically lower wages while increasing profits. (Does any of this sound familiar? Recently?)

Those who remained employed earned about nine bucks a week for a 56-hour week. In some companies, half of the workforce was composed of girls 14-18 years of age. Among the working families, child mortality and adult mortality rates were staggering, with 50% of children dead before reaching 6, and well over 1/3 of adult workers dying by age 25. Charming, simply charming.

In one of the defining moments of the early 20th century, textile workers – complaining of low wages and bad working conditions – took to the streets. The owners, and the local government responded with brutal force, sending in police and militia. Only when the resulting savagery, including beatings of women and children, received widespread press coverage across the country did the owners back off.

As the labor movement continued to organize against this kind of unfair exploitation, many owners came to realize that without a workforce, industry would grind to a halt – creating a lose-lose. Roosevelt was a major player in bringing about a compromise, and an uneasy truce between labor and capitalists was reached. With various ups and downs, that truce largely endured for the better part of a century.

Now let me be clear that I am far from a cheerleader for organized labor. When conditions such as those in Lawrence were created, the unions were essential, and in fact as Henry Ford understood, decent pay for decent work in safe conditions ultimately resulted in a large middle class – which in turn created a market for Ford's automobiles and for other American products and services. A genuine win-win.

However, at times, militant labor became not just a substantial cost component of production, but also an impediment to new methods and equipment, and an impediment to practical steps that would keep industry in the U.S. competitive. Many of the labor unions became pawns of organized criminals, who were looking for new rackets to replace their lucrative liquor trade with the end of prohibition.

Many labor leaders climbed to the top, driven not by any concern for their members, but by the power, perks, and payoffs – by a level of greed and hunger for power that was every bit as vicious as the worst of the Capitalists.

The novelist Ayn Rand, fugitive from the communist takeover in Russia, cast such greedy and power hungry union leaders as villains in her novels. And she was right about the problem they posed, right about their motives, and had direct experience of the debilitating destruction of society that could result from the communist pipe dream.

But it is hard to keep a canoe upright when you stand completely on one side or the other. Even in 2012, when one looks at the reader comments that follow reasonable and intelligent news articles, the epitaph "communist" and "socialist" is hurled at anyone who suggests the slightest modification or control of laissez-faire capitalism.

Marx thought his vision was inevitable, and worked to make it so. Unfortunately for all of us, what he really did was hand to a subset of 20th century capitalists, what I call the "Nouveaux Capitalistes", the smoke-making machine to hide from view their plans to get very, very rich with relatively little effort, at your and my expense.

Maybe this is a good time to remember Buffett's warning: "There's class warfare, all right, but it's my class, the rich class, that's making war, and we're winning."

Now a big part of the smoke screen relates to who is losing in this. If you are not in the 47% of the U.S. who, judging by recent campaign rhetoric, are "deadbeats, lay-abouts, and pay no taxes", y'all got nothin' to worry about. Not.

Do the math. The U.S. debt, for example, belongs to y'all. And who is that debt actually owed to? Why to the same 0.001% that took all of the money off the table already. Now it comes to a point where they've taken the last drop of blood from the middle class. But like all vampires, they are still hungry. So who is next for lunch? Got a few hundred grand or a couple of million in the bank? We'll be around for lunch next month.

Notes:

_____

_____

_____

_____

_____

_____

_____

_____

_____

"Mere anarchy is loosed upon the world,
The blood-dimmed tide is loosed, and everywhere
The ceremony of innocence is drowned;
The best lack all conviction, while the worst
Are full of passionate intensity.
...
And what rough beast, its hour come round at last,
Slouches towards Bethlehem to be born?"

(William Butler Yeats - "The Second Coming")

Chapter 6 – New Capitalists and the Destruction of America

So after fifty years of looking for a communist under the bed, it turns out the real danger is the vampire in the closet. Who'd a thunk it?

Well, you are not really supposed to catch on, and the smoke screens and the messages are carefully controlled to make sure you don't. In earlier days, information was controlled, information traveled slowly, and history was relatively easy to manipulate.

The slow speed at which information traveled was both a curse and a blessing, as to an extent it limited the damage that could be inflicted in a short time. So Cooley's argument that technology has been a big factor in the recent wealth transfer is actually correct, but by a totally different set of mechanisms and for totally different reasons than he has proposed. We will see how this plays out in chapter 9.

Who is this "sub-class" of capitalists, and how are they different from Henry Ford, John Deere, and George Eastman during the period of American industrial expansion? Very simple, really. Most of the New Capitalists are not builders, but destroyers. Rather than jobs, opportunities, growth, and innovation, the New Capitalists leave behind them empty factories, and broken dreams.

In terms of sheer numbers, most are people who *play games with money*. Why bother with actually working to build stuff, if you can get richer faster just playing with money? Now this was not an attitude shared by Capitalists like Ford, and Eastman, and Hewlett, and Packard, who liked to build stuff, and who built companies intended to last.

It is the growth of this subclass of New Capitalist "money players" that makes a lie of the "trickle-down theory of wealth"; the theory still trumpeted by politicians today that money in the hands of the rich will magically lead to new industry and new jobs. It is simply not working that way in 2012.

The people who focus primarily on money include those who lend it, those who gamble with it, and those who manipulate it. It also includes people who started out on the other side, as builders, but finding their building talents not equal to their vampire appetite for lucre, turn their talents to extracting money in a vicious "I win - you lose" game for very high stakes.

For the people who play these games, the fact that other people could lose their livelihood, lose their homes, or even lose their life really does not seem to matter very much. "I'm all right Jack."

The Barbarians

The worst are modern day Barbarians, totally unconstrained by any kind of ethics or character; people and companies who will rape, pillage, and murder or sponsor rape, pillage, and murder – as long as the money rolls in. Like King Leopold of Belgium did in the Congo early in the 20th century.

These Barbarians will also promote products that they know are dangerous, or consort to corner and control the market. They encourage warfare, as one of the quickest ways to get rich. A few hundred thousand dead? So what? I have my Rolls, my trophy bride, my yacht, my wine cellars in my five mansions – I'm good!

Andrew Harvey, in his inspiring book The Hope, describes a luncheon conversation in the early '90s with an unnamed man on the fringe of meetings preparing for the U.N. Environment and Development conference in Rio. The well-dressed stranger introduced himself as the head of a major agribusiness corporation. Harvey relates the exposition (one can't call it a conversation) over a page and a half. Two short excerpts:

> "I know exactly what my company is doing, and the devastation it is causing to thousands of lives.... I know, and I do not care."

> "I know too that none of my shareholders care a rat's ass what I do, or how I do it, providing I keep them swimming in cash" (The Hope, p 174)

Those who knowingly consort with such Barbarians are the worst kind of hypocrites, and willing accessories to murder. The Barbarians include several multinational corporations who are household names in the U.S. And they will sell out an entire country in a heartbeat.

There is a dissonance that sets in, because most decent honest and hard-working people, which is the majority of humanity, have been taught to honor and look up to the wealthy – to the "successful".

It is therefore hard for most of us to even imagine that people like this exist, scum that must be described as evil, and that this scum controls companies that are engaged in activities that are evil.

You or I might well own some of these companies' stock in our portfolios, being either blissfully unaware of their actions, or unaware that we even own the stock – because it is held in a pension plan or mutual fund, run by fund managers who see their job as keeping us "swimming in cash".

The accumulation of wealth that results also means an accumulation of power, and with that comes influence. Swells with a few million of loose change in their pocket have access to the political establishment that is denied the lower and middle class. That means that they can influence government in ways that advantage them.

> "I am under no illusion that I will not someday have to pay the price….I'm willing to pay that price in return for the pleasure of being able to afford this restaurant, in return for being able to ring up the president of the United States in front of house guests to impress them. Am I getting through to you?"
> (The Hope, p 175)

American Legislative Exchange Council

Sometimes evil works alone, and sometimes evil goes really big. The grand alliance of big business and politicians – the American Legislative Exchange Council (ALEC) is the most organized and insidious such group – formed during the glory years of Ronald Reagan – and responsible for literally hundreds of State bills that have been – to put it mildly, "business friendly". Now let me be clear here. By business friendly I don't mean jobs, I mean massive profits – almost always at the public's expense.

Writing in 1776, Adam Smith put it this way:

> "The proposal of any new law or regulation of commerce which comes from this order, ought always to be listened to with great precaution, and ought never to be adopted till after having been long and carefully examined, not only with the most scrupulous, but with the most suspicious attention. It comes from an order of men, whose interest is never exactly the same with that of the public, who have

generally an interest to deceive and even to oppress the public, and who accordingly have, upon many occasions, both deceived and oppressed it."

Plus ça change, plus c'est la même chose.

Now occasionally in the past when the smell became too strong, "we the people" have pressured governments to enact legislation to control the more outrageous activities of this vampire class, but then vampires live forever. When things get tough, they duck into their fancy castles, and re-emerge with the next full moon or violent storm.

It is relatively easy to discern how modifications to the laws of the land intended to benefit business have occurred shortly before every single serious downturn in the economy. And then the vampires emerged to feed. When certain factors – some controlled or manipulated by the new capitalists – lead to "the perfect storm", we get a market crash that can be disastrous and long lasting, and bring untold misery to tens of thousands, while bringing fantastic profits to a chosen few.

This is generally followed by retroactive analysis by politicians of what happened, and legislation to mitigate against it happening in future, also popularly known as "locking the barn door after the horse is out". Then, depending on the depth of the destruction, follows a period of relative calm – and forgetting. Failing to learn from history, we repeat it, and the games continue.

Notes:

_____

_____

_____

_____

_____

It takes 20 years to build a reputation and five minutes to ruin it. If you think about that, you'll do things differently....

It's better to hang out with people better than you. Pick out associates whose behavior is better than yours and you'll drift in that direction.
(Warren Buffett, from "www.brainyquote.com")

Chapter 7 – The Role of the Securities Market

The role of "the market' in all of this is very simple. Early old money went to finance various ventures and adventures, from trading spices in the East Indies to arguing that the earth was not really flat and that India could be reached from the Atlantic side. But to finance and equip a voyage of discovery or of pillage was an expensive undertaking, so usually required that one know people with "real" money. Kings were good for this.

Loans were an option, but convincing bankers to part with large amounts of money on "speculation" was difficult – at least it was in those days. And if one ran up a debt that could not be paid, the reward was debtor's prison, not just for the debtor, but also for his wife and children.

So one looked first to family and friends. They were offered a "share" in the profits of the venture, and encouraged to fund it. Since stiffing Aunt Matilda was generally frowned upon, these transactions tended to be reasonably gentile – for the times.

Having wealthy friends increased one's opportunities, so certain social practices encouraged mingling among the wealthy. (Today we have country clubs and squash courts.) As the demands for capital became more and more extensive, other mechanisms were required.

And so was born the stock market. The Web provides a huge resource of well-organized information about the stock market on Investopedia. Suffice it for our purposes to say that the concept of sharing in the funding, and receiving dividends for participation arose sometime in the 1600's.

It did not take long for the practice of issuing and selling shares to attract people who were into get-rich-quick and/or win-lose. In fact the issuing of "shares" was banned in Britain after the South Seas Bubble crash of 1720, and selling shares was not legal in Britain until after 1825.

Meanwhile, the NYSE was formed in 1792, making its home on Wall Street. If you are trying to raise money for a risky venture, the really nice thing about the stock market is that you are now dealing with complete strangers, through a group of middlemen called brokers. A nice side effect of this arrangement is that you do not have to worry anymore about stiffing Aunt Matilda. The investors are complete strangers, so not of any real consequence.

Bonds vs. Stocks

So bond issues and dividend bearing stocks, and actual participating shares in the enterprise became the name of the game. The difference between bonds and stocks can be considered this way: you can own the money, and take a percent on it, or you can own a "share" of the company and its' profits. For risky ventures, a shareholder shared both the risk and the reward, while the bondholder settled in advance for a fixed percentage on his investment.

As the mercantile trade gave way to the fruits of industrialization, the focus on sharing in any particular "Treasure Island" gave way to long-term investments based on growth of manufacturing, or development of infrastructure such as railways, and in the sharing of long-term profits, through dividends.

Dividends are money paid out from surplus profits, after taxes, that the company decides it does not need to reserve for ongoing operations. The surplus is paid back to shareholders as a fixed dollar amount for each share held.

Liquidity and Volatility

If you did not want to wait for that long-term thing to materialize, you might have decided to sell your shares at some point. To do so, you needed a buyer.

This is the concept of liquidity – which means if I want to sell, there is a buyer out there somewhere who will give me money to take over "my position" – to buy my shares at whatever the perceived value is at the time. If no one wants to buy, or if someone will buy only at a substantial discount over what I think the shares are worth, I have a problem. I might have to sell my shares well below the current market price, and that sale then establishes a new price for the shares on the market.

For thinly traded stocks – stocks that don't have a large number of buyers and sellers, these transactions can lead to high price volatility. Small numbers of shares change hands and the price bounces around from day to day. It is rather like being on a roller coaster.

High volatility in thinly traded stocks is both expected and of no real concern to the market overall. But when high trading **volumes** accompany high volatility, and the volatility spreads across a substantial number of stocks, even in a single sector of the market – say textiles, or "dot coms" for example – the consequences can be very nasty. Think 1929-32, 2001-2002, and 2007-2009.

In the early days, the rules of this "securities" game were somewhat loosey-goosey, and one's money was often anything but "secure". Various governments tried to act in the public interest, and provide some structure and rules of play, but it seems the wealthy capitalists and their henchmen, the brokers, were often one step ahead.

(I often wonder if brokers were so named for their skill in making the unwary go broke.)

The wealthiest business owners, from an early age, also have had the resources and connections to influence the government of the day. This has resulted in legislation and counter-legislation at various times in history that played a large part in stabilizing or destabilizing the markets. When new proposed legislation becomes contentious, volatility goes up. One of the key causes of the crash of 1929 was the large volatility in the market caused by the protectionist Smoot-Hawley bill.

Then there was the Commodity Futures Modernization Act of 2000 – the single source of most of the market turmoil of this decade.

Steve Minter, in his Industry Week article: "Did American Capitalism Take a Wrong Turn?" clearly points to increased lobbying by business interests starting in the 1970s, as the point where things start to go off the rails. The American Legislative Exchange Council formed in the 80's was a natural extension of that effort.

We will return to government in a later chapter, but first let's see how the securities market plays into the larger picture.

Notes:

_____

_____

_____

_____

_____

_____

"…But the hands of the have nots, keep falling out of reach. Black day in July."
(Gordon Lightfoot, "Black Day in July", 1968)

Chapter 8 – Diagnosing Market Problems

The 5S games of the securities market have contributed in a large measure to getting us into the mess we are in. This is a huge problem, because the orderly flow of capital combined with a large and stable middle-class are two fundamental keys to life, liberty, and the pursuit of happiness.

If 80-90% of all of the people in the world could be truly part of the "middle class", with modest homes, small families, decent food, clean water, open educational opportunities, and good health care, would there be war? Would the U.S. have to spend 25% of its total budget on a combination of prisons, security, and the military? When is the last time you saw a bunch of soccer moms and dads take lead pipes, firebombs, and machetes to mix it up in the neighborhood on the next block, or in the next town?

Is this a utopian dream? Yes it is. John Lennon, arguably one of the most inspiring and poetic singer-songwriters of recent time (like Lightfoot in his heyday), penned these famous lines in 1971 – at the height of the Vietnam war.

> "…you may say
> I'm a dreamer, but I'm not the only one
> I hope some day you'll join us
> And the world will be as one."

The rest of Lennon's lyrics cross the line for some folks – when he talks about "no countries", "no possessions", and "no religion". But maybe if we could constrain the really negative affects of countries, possessions, and religion, then we could focus on what I, in my "John Lennon" or "Gordon Lightfoot" moments, see as the key issues:

> "No need for greed or hunger
> A brotherhood of man"

From where I sit, there are two choices that mankind can take. Behind door number one: a road that slowly gets us closer to that world that Lennon describes, or behind door number two: a road to increasing anarchy, destruction, slavery, and misery. We are at a choice point. I know which door I choose, and "I hope someday you will join us ...", like, maybe starting now.

But to get there, we need to engage in "continuous improvement". Just as manufacturing companies embark on a program that is ongoing and never ending to become the best company they can, we need as humankind to set out on the "Lean journey" to become the best we can. Of course we have to believe this is really possible. I am a dreamer, and in this I dream Big.

The Value Stream Caveat

There are three big themes in Lean thinking. The first big idea is that we should seek to provide value for the customer, and should listen to the **voice of the customer**, who will tell us what they value if we choose to listen.

The second big idea is that to fix problems permanently, you need to get at **the root cause** of the problem and fix that, rather than putting band-aids on symptoms of the problem.

And the third big idea is that analyzing and fixing the system that provides value for the customer – fixing the value stream and planning for a new future state or future vision – is a TEAM activity, not something done in an Oval office or a back room by one or two people.

So I am throwing out some ideas here regarding what I see as the customer values, the problems, the root causes, and how I think we could begin to fix them. I am putting colored sticky notes on the value stream map.

Because this is a team exercise, you must add your own sticky notes, which can of course negate mine. You can negate my ideas, and other's ideas only by adding your own – that is, you can provide a diametrically opposed root problem definition or problem solution – but you can't take down my ideas or those of anyone else. One of the rules of engagement for this team play is that no one can arbitrarily take down other people's sticky notes.

The way it works is this. We have pads of "sticky notes" in three different colors:

- Yellow is for recording "root cause" for a particular problem.
- Blue is for recording "possible solutions", individual steps we might take.
- Green is for recording "how" questions, because some solutions will not be easy to implement. They might need additional analysis or new metrics.

If we were all sitting in a circle in the decision process, we would speak further to our notes, discussing why we see thing in a particular way. Because I am reaching out in print medium, I sometimes need to provide these addenda on the written page as my notes for the team meeting.

Collect all the ideas – all the value descriptions, all the wastes, all the root causes, and then make some **team** decisions on solutions. They all stay posted and visible. They all stay in play, until the team analyses, compares, splits, merges and finally decides which are the most productive ideas to implement.

So after this long-winded preamble, we are ready to talk about the 5S games of the securities biz. And remind yourself continually that what is going on in one game league definitely interacts in serious ways with what is happening in another. That's how one builds (and sometimes uses for personal gain) the perfect storm.

Let the games begin. Having been on the subject of brokers, we will start with the Shill Game.

Because I am not one to "walk on eggs" around complex topics, instead I will be stomping on eggs. So there is a big egg-colored warning label on the following material: "Danger Ahead – One Dude's Opinion." You need to add your own opinion and data.

Let's stomp some securities eggs!

Notes:

_____

_____

_____

_____

_____

_____

_____

_____

_____

_____

_____

_____

_____

"Those who lead the company, however, were born public relations directors, who set up offices furnished with affluence in the most extravagant quarters. People, once they saw the wealth the SSC was "generating," couldn't keep their money from gravitating towards the SSC."
(Investopedia – about "The South Sea Bubble of 1711")

Chapter 9 – The Shill Game

We have all at one time in our lives probably visited the circus midway, where a barker, standing at the entrance of a big tent from which emanates mysterious music and strange sounds, invites us to see the "Beast of the Jungle Turn into a Beautiful Woman" or some such equivalent "wonder". Scattered though the crowd are the Shills, each of whom pretends to be just another visitor and talks it up - or in the case of games of chance, shows us how easy it is to win, win, WIN!

In many companies in today's corporate world, we call the "barker" the CEO. His job is not really to run the company. In fact, he is much too frequently hired into a company where he has zero expertise in what that company actually produces – and frequently demonstrates that fact! But actually running the company is not his "real job". His real job is to get the suckers to hand over their money to keep the lights burning. Does this characterize all CEOs? Most certainly not! Is it true of some? You betcha!

Now the "shills" in the game mainly live in a special and equally mysterious big tent called "Wall Street". In business terms, they are called brokers, and their job is to convince you that the CEO really does have something worthwhile behind the curtain or inside the kimono. And they get a cut of the profits for every sucker they can line up. But unlike the midway shills, brokers get paid both coming and going.

In fact, the more erratic a company's performance is, the more money they make. Without high "volatility", brokers can't make very much through simple buy-order commissions. So over time they have put their collective heads together, and come up with and/or promoted a whole bunch of schemes to increase their take. One of these is "short selling", which is the subject of a later chapter. Another scheme is derivatives. For the rest of us, this is a Standardized way to get Poor, for which we can use the shorthand S&P.

Volatility and Brokers

Is it in the best interest of the investor to buy a good solid stock, with really good upside, and maybe dividends, and then hold it for a long time? Seems to me that is what the market should be about, and has been at various times in history. Rather like a marriage intended to last. This is called buy and hold.

If I could have bought stock in Microsoft when Bill Gates was still working out of his basement (I have a 1980's Byte Magazine with his personal telephone number), and I held that stock until today, when Microsoft is (finally) giving dividends (mostly 'cause they don't know what else to do with all of that moola), I should have made a LOT of money. But my broker would have made squat!

Brokers like volatility. Every trade brings them money. The more trades, the more money. This is not rocket science. Conversely, buy and hold does not make them money.

Brokers don't like making "squat", so they have to convince me to get a divorce. If they can get me to sell, they get a piece, and then of course they get a piece from the new buyer as well. Nice. Clean. Easy money.

Do they really care if the stock goes up or down? Good question. In fairness, I have had some good brokers, people who worked hard for me and tried to help me make money in the market. Are they in the majority? I'm not convinced. So how does this work?

(Ring!) Hey John, I have a hot one! Ready to really break out! Yeah, the sector is booming. They do (fill in the blank). Big upside! Yeah, been watching this one for quite a while. *(Translation – I myself bought stock in this when it was 10 cents a share)*. Yeah! Think I can get you in at $1.10. Thousand shares? You got it!

(Ring!) Hey Sally, I have a hot one!… Yeah! Think I can get you in at $2.20. How many? Great! Good move.

(Ring!) Hey John. You been watching that stock in (fill in the blank)? Seems to be slipping in the numbers. Don't know where it will end up. I recommend we move you to (fill in the blank). *(Translation – I originally bought a cheap stock for 10 cents a share that I was later able to sell for $4 a share, 'cause I convinced the suckers there was really something under the kimono. A few people are starting to get suspicious about the upside, so I have liquidated my position, pocketed the cash and it is now time to bid up my next hot stock.)*

Investment Banks, (New) Old Games, and Technology

Now this gets particularly gnarly when not just individual brokers but brokerage firms also "take a position" in the stocks they are pushing. This should be prohibited by morality. This should be prohibited by law. But it isn't. When banking institutions get into this game, through brokerage arms or investment banks that promote the same companies that the bankers are debt financing, things really get twisted out of shape.

This was illegal from 1933 until 1999. Basically the gap between serious market crashes. What a coincidence! If you are interested in the actual details, look up the "Glass-Steagall Act", which erected a "wall" between investment banks and commercial banks in 1933, and the "Gramm-Leach-Bliley" Act of 1999, which removed that wall.

Aside: Since part of the "spin" in the 2012 election was that this 1999 bill was signed by Democrat Clinton, it is perhaps useful to note that the co-sponsors of the "Gramm-Leach-Bliley" Act were Sen. Phil Gramm (R, Texas), Rep. Jim Leach (R, Iowa), and Rep. Thomas J. Bliley, Jr. (R, Virginia).

*When I pointed this out on a discussion group, I was told in no uncertain terms that "Yes, but President Clinton changed the bill." Of course for the President to **change** a bill is not permissible under the constitution. And Sen. Phil Gramm's name will come up again.*

The Shill Game reached new heights in the 1990's, and technology played a big role. Remember that Cooley said technology was a big factor in the transfer of wealth away from the middle class. We discussed this in chapter one. He is absolutely right about the what. It is just his explanation of "how" technology caused this that I take exception to.

Several things came together to create a perfect storm in the 1990s. First there was the systematic dismantling of the Glass-Steagall Act of 1933 that seriously gained steam on Ronald Reagan's watch, with tremendous help from the Fed under Greenspan, and was completed by a Republican Congress in the dying days of the Clinton Presidency. This culminated with the passage and signing of the Financial Services Modernization Act of 1999, as the "Gramm-Leach-Bliley" Act is also called.

Second was the nature of innovation at the time, with the dot-com buzz around both technologies and business models that most investors did not understand, and for which they had no workable metrics to measure real potential. To put this in context, the Internet got up to speed only in 1994. But brokers talked these stocks up, and up, and UP. *(Ring!)*

Third was the entry into the market of very large numbers of on-line traders, who could directly place buy and sell orders from the comfort of their home or office. In fact, between 1999 and 2000, 2.2 million **additional** households began investing online, bringing the total online investing households to over 3 Million.

These online traders could also place "sell stops" to limit loses if stocks fell below a certain point. Sell stops automatically issue a "sell" order if the price of a stock falls below a certain point. This tool is used by serious investors to make sure they don't get caught by an unexpected price decline. Sounds good, until you figure out how this plays out in the "Short Game".

Fourth was the growth of a subset of on-line traders, the so-called "day traders", who were into and back out of stocks on the same day. Now this is the very antithesis of capitalists like Henry Ford, or Aunt Sarah with her AT&T shares stored under her needlepoint. This is not about building factories and jobs. This is about being a "quick buck" artist.

And the technological tools at the disposal of a day trader are incredible. Live feeds, instant visibility into buy-sell orders, real-time visibility of technical data on market direction or "sentiment". Enough technology, computers, monitors, and TVs to be the situation room for the Iraq War – and it does not add value. It is a shoot-em-up computer game, a game that makes real money, but does not add value to the economy.

And fifth and possibly the most important addition to the Shill Game – the Stock Advice Guru, coming to your inbox with the latest hot product. I don't know about you, but I get probably a dozen of these every single day – "psssst. I got a look under the Kimono. Hot, hot, hot."

Cracking Some Shilling Eggs

Yellow Sticky Note: Root problem – Misrepresentation of value.

Blue Sticky Note: Proposed solution – Punish shills who knowingly lie, or who primarily use "shilling" to drive up the price of stocks that they personally own.

My Notes for the Team Meeting: There is this thing in the consumer market called "truth in advertising" which prohibits by law unfair, deceptive, untrue or misleading advertising resulting in injury, lost money, or lost property. The normal remedy is full restitution, with costs.

Yellow Sticky Note: Root problem – Pay for service (buy/sell commission) promotes bad broker behavior.

Blue Sticky Note: Proposed solution – Pay for performance.

My Notes for the Team Meeting: This is a huge egg, and if we crack it, then the creatures inside will scream like hell. But I put it to you this way. When I trade my own stocks, using a computerized system for the purpose, my cost per trade should be based on the real cost amortized over the whole system and all users. This should really be pennies, not the exorbitant fees I actually have to pay for my own on-line trades. And I win or lose (assuming the game is not rigged) by how informed I am as an investor.

When I have a broker, who is supposed to know the stocks he is recommending and be watching my back all the time, then I should be paying for that service. So what is the service? Is it pushing the keys to make a trade, which costs pennies, or is it understanding the market and making money for me through good advice. Would I happily pay a professional broker 10% or even 15% of my gains? Sure. Notice that this change would create a capitalist model where the broker makes money because he has skin in the game.

Brokers right now follow a much more socialist model, where they get paid even if they are lousy at what they do. That is, unless they want to define themselves as shills, who fall over themselves to make more than any other shill on the block, by lining up the most suckers and squeezing them dry in the least amount of time.

So if you live inside this egg, before you scream like hell, look in the mirror and be honest with yourself – are you a professional broker of services, or are you behaving like a shill? And could you make an honest living from a 10-15% commission on 80% of your trades?

Bad Business Behaviours

In and of itself, the Shill Game would not cost the economy tooooo big. Some brokers would pocket a big chunk in sales commissions, but otherwise, maybe it's not a big deal.

But what makes it a big deal is that it almost universally drives bad behavior in businesses as well. This can be simple wasteful behavior, as further described in this chapter, or can extend to outright fraud – which is the subject of Chapter 12.

What has changed in the capitalist model in the last hundred years? One fundamental change has been in the role of capital and its' impact on business behavior. Let's suppose I had started a company, say in 1933. I did the "friends and family thing", then got the promoters on side, and raised a bunch of money to start building out my dream for company X.

Investors settled for financial results – compiled with paper and pencil, or later mechanical adding machines – sometime in the 6 months following yearend. General communication to the overall public about the financial status of my company was very limited.

Since my objective in 1933 was to build the company, I concentrated on activities that would make that happen, and did not concern myself all that much with what the stock price was doing at any particular time. The short-term stock price would be an issue only if I wanted to expand company X faster than cash flow from operations would allow, and therefore needed to raise additional capital.

Fast forward to 2000. My company X is gianormous. In fact, it is not my company anymore. It now belongs to thousands of investors – often represented by brokerage firms on the board of directors – and to C-level management and Directors who are excessively well paid. But more important to this narrative, these C-level management and Directors count on stock options to join the ranks of the super-rich.

I've long ago been forced out by machinations in the board, and have gone off to start something new. (Think Steve Jobs or Jack Tramiel, for example.) And company X has tens or hundreds of thousands of employees.

Everybody and their dog has access to financial information about company X. It is reported in almost real time, with thousands of lines of accounts, transactions, and reports accessible to a cadre of Shills who use this to build their pitch. Instead of the numbers from last fiscal year, delayed 6 months, now everyone hangs on the numbers **this** quarter, available literally hours past the quarter end. Wonders of technology – that technology that Cooley talked about!

How does this encourage wasteful or bad behavior? Ever try to talk to anyone in manufacturing around quarter end? I have. In my B2B, I talk to people a lot. "Hi Tom, I was wondering how the decision on …..Oh, sorry, forgot it was your quarter end! I'll call back next week when things are back to normal."

If you are a CEO, the market demands you make your numbers for the quarter, and quarterly forecasts are the stuff of dreams … and nightmares. A few bucks up or down, and your stock can soar like an eagle, or hit the pavement like a dead skunk. So C-level execs drive employees to get those orders out the door before end of quarter, so they can book the receivables to make their quarter-end numbers.

In high tech, it is not unusual for engineers to be pulled off research that is critical to next-gen products to help out on the factory floor – operating the equipment or even carrying boxes. I'm kidding, right? Not. If you have friends or neighbors in the manufacturing biz, ask for their take on "quarter-end".

[Of course with the massive outsourcing of manufacturing that has occurred since 2000, actually finding a company, particularly in high tech, that manufactures the products they sell is something of a challenge.]

This quarter-end-crunch behavior violates all the rules they teach in Lean Manufacturing and Six-Sigma classes about providing value to customers by evening out product flow. It impacts price stability, as companies resort to quarter-end discounting. It impacts quality, as rushed volume leads to higher error rates, and it leads to ripples through the supply chain. I call this "yo-yo" production, because volumes and prices bounce up and down like a yo-yo. This is waste generating, and does not provide the best value for customers.

But quarter-end madness isn't about value for customers. It's about **appearing** to provide value for **shareholders** in order to keep that stock price up. This pressure to make the numbers can also drive other behaviors that cross the line from wasteful to criminal, as we will see in the Shell game.

Yellow Sticky Note: Root problem – The quarter-end-numbers effect, which includes the entire set of bad behaviors: shifting resources, receivables, payables, and labor to make the quarter-end numbers look better to investors – a.k.a. the yo-yo effect.

Blue Sticky Note: Proposed solution – Hire C-levels who actually understand the business they are in, who plan to stay in the business for the long haul because they believe in what they are doing, and who have the honesty, public-relations skills, and communications skills to lay it on the line to investors about the market, the product, and the timelines to any particular level of returns.

Blue Sticky Note: Proposed solution – Watch companies whose quarter end sales are way out of whack with the rest of the quarter, or the next quarter, whose sales and production bounce up and down like a yo-yo, and don't invest in them.

Blue Sticky Note: Look at C-Level compensation and find ways to decouple this from short-term market moves and short-term profit numbers.

Green Sticky Note: Do we need to change broker behavior too? How can we do that?

My Notes for the Team Meeting: Yo-yos create yo-yos. It is not physically possible to maintain Lean processes (including Lean inventory) if your whole operation is one big yo-yo. If you, the reader, are a Lean process consultant, you know exactly what I am talking about, and how yo-yo production builds in waste at every level of the operation.

It also sets up yo-yo ripple effects that radiate out through the entire supply chain, and puts yo-yo demand on capital requirements. So part of the solution truly is, if you don't want yo-yo production, don't hire yo-yos at the C-level to run it!

If the reader is not a Lean process consultant, which most probably are not, you might need to trust me on this one.

Green Sticky Note: For all you business statisticians out there, how could we develop a "yo-yo production" measure, which, with a simple index, would let us rank company A against company B on the long term "yo-yo" scale? This might be a lot more useful than moving averages, which measure "sentiment". (Not that "sentiment" is not real – it just represents a statistical best guess based on stock price, **not** on company performance.)

The Load-em Up Gambit

Manufacturers are a part of the total supply chain, often working through dealers, who in turn sell the product to the end-user. The auto-biz is a good example of that. Sitting on dealers' lots are huge inventories of vehicles purchased from the manufacturer, and often financed by the money arm of the OEM manufacturer though "floor-plan financing"

This is good for the OEM, because it pushes more product out the door and improves the quarterly numbers. And the financial arm is making interest on the dealer loan. But if more and more dealers are loaded up with more and more inventory – and that inventory is not moving off the lot – trouble is brewing in River City.

Unsold inventory is never a good thing. It is not an asset, even though that is where accountants put it when they do the books. If the product does not make it to the final end-user customer, but sits in the manufacture's warehouse, or on the dealer lot, it is really a ticking time bomb.

When the markets bottomed out in 2002, telecommunications giant Cisco wrote off over $2 Billion dollars worth of equipment they had manufactured and could not sell. In the 2008 meltdown, one of the effects was closure of nearly 3800 car dealerships.

As VP Product Management for a small company in 1997 that was aiming for an initial public offering (IPO), I saw the "load-em-up" game working up close and personal. I learned a lot about business from my CEO, most of it good. But one exception was that he also played the "load-em-up" game, requiring new dealers to stock a substantial amount of product, which boosted our numbers immediately, but left the dealer on the hook. This was machinated via the VP Sales, so was outside my bailiwick.

Now the theory here is that the dealer, having sunk the money in the inventory, has more incentive to sell. If you also promise to deliver additional complementary product, it sounds not so bad, unless your promises don't match the reality of what is practical. (This is called "product overhang" in the biz. There's a not-inconsequential amount of Shilling involved in most sales processes too.) The biggest problem is that you can start viewing your dealers as your customers, rather than as your partners.

We soon had some annoyed dealers out there, one of whom was in Silicon Valley, with lots of moneyed connections. Add in a ticked-off former employee (former because he did not make his quarter-end numbers), and within a matter of months we had a new competitor, sitting in the heart of our potential market.

By the middle of that year, our company was heading in a different product direction in pursuit of a workable IPO strategy – a product direction that was of less personal interest to me but had more "dot.com" appeal – so my wife and I bought the rights to the current products and went on our own.

That left the dealer network to us, and one of our first tasks was to fire up the channel. When we approached the companies that had been on the receiving end of previous dealer negotiations, we got an earful! Suffice it to say, we had to build our own dealer network – starting from scratch.

The Taj Mahal Effect

Another type of bad behavior I call the Taj Mahal Effect, in which huge amounts of money, generally leveraged though debt financing, goes into the construction of massively expensive real estate which is "just occasionally" overkill for the purpose.

Don't get me wrong. Companies need decent space to carry on their work, and bright, spacious, and airy surroundings are good for morale and can contribute to better work habits. I've seen that in my own small company.

But they don't need to be the modern day Taj Mahal – **unless their function is primarily to impress investors and potential customers.** (Remember the "South Seas Bubble" quote at the beginning of this chapter?)

I saw the Taj Mahal effect in spades here in "Silicon Valley North" during the height of the dot.com rush. Just before Nortel crashed and burned, they built a 330,000 square foot state-of-the-art factory on Palladium drive to meet with growing (projected?) demand for their telecom products.

Now granted they needed class 100 and higher clean room capability, so just any old factory would not do, but at a time when there were already some signs and predictions that the waters ahead might get choppy, this facility was – in my opinion – overkill.

It was financed and built, equipment was ordered and installed, and commissioning was underway. I toured parts of it with my then 20-year old daughter, who was employed as a trainer for some of the state-of-the-art wafer testing equipment.

But before the first real product could be produced, the entire facility was on the block. Brand new highly specialized production equipment was on fire sale for 10 cents on the dollar. Since there were few local buyers for that kind of stuff, my guess is that most of that equipment ended up in Asia. Over thirty thousand Nortel employees became ex-Nortel employees.

Nortel was just one of many. I picked up some super bargains in brand new just-out-of-the-box office chairs from a building down the street when a start-up went bust in much the same way, leaving a fancy new building and lots of office equipment.

Awash with Venture Capital, companies just could not seem to avoid trying to project "prosperity" by building fancy digs, rather than putting the money toward R&D or systematic improvements in production.

Fast forward to 2010. The renewables sector is hot. A company with some very neat and patented technology has attracted about $200 Million in private investment capital and another $535 Million in Federal loan guarantees that were a part of the Bush Energy Policy Act of 2005.

In spite of pressure from the Bush administration to fast track the loan approval prior to tuning over the reigns to the Democrats, the Department of Energy credit review committee, which consisted of career civil servants with financial expertise, delayed approval for another six months as part of a due-diligence process.

When the funds were finally in hand, Solyndra built a new fab, costing $733 Million, employing over 3000 people in the construction, and completed on time and on budget. The plan was to get production capacity to 610 megawatts by 2013 – but they soon closed their old Fab 1, and concentrated all production at Fab 2. By August of the following year they filed for bankruptcy protection, laid off 1100 employees, and shut down all manufacturing.

While there has been a tremendous amount of smoke associated with this particular venture, a full review of the timelines and actions taken by both the White House and the Department of Energy over a three-year approval process suggests that there was no impropriety of any kind. But the politics that arose around it, actually sealed Solyndra's fate.

Does Solyndra deserve criticism for a level of misjudgment of the market, and for failing to anticipate a 50% drop in conventional panel prices driven by ramped up state-supported production in China? This is an open question. The Communist-Chinese government support by has been widely described as a deliberate plot to destroy the nascent American solar manufacturing industry before it could get up any steam.

But Solyndra has been criticized, and I believe legitimately criticized, for committing resources of $733 million from $200 Million in private investment capital and another $535 Million in Federal loan guarantees to a Taj Mahal, rather than immediately committing these resources to optimize production and to get the cost-per-watt down, while managing in less fancy digs.

Many companies have been similarly criticized for spending large amounts on glass and steel "headquarters" buildings, where the corporate elite can be safely isolated from the grubby folks who actually make stuff.

Yellow Sticky Note: Root problem – Taj Mahal mentality.

Blue Sticky Note: Proposed solution – To customers and investors: Don't be dazzled by the digs.

My Notes for the Team Meeting: For a customer or investor, the Taj Mahal should be a really bad sign. It means the company knows how to spend money, but that does not correlate with knowing how to make money, and is generally negatively correlated with knowing how to save money.

If you are a customer planning to buy from a company, and the front entrance has enough room to bivouac a division of Marines, then they charge too much (… unless they actually **do** rent it out on the weekend to the Marine Corp. ….You could ask!)

If you are an investor, or potential investor, ask, "Whose money built all this, and how does it deliver customer value?"

Green Sticky Note: Is there a negative correlation between variable A – the actual size and physical separation of the CEO's corner office from the real working parts of the company such as the engineering offices and production floor, and variable B – the companies performance?

My Notes for the Team Meeting: I ask because I think there is a negative correlation, and this might be useful data to collect. Sergio Marchionne, CEO of Fiat-Chrysler is reported to have abandoned the former CEO office at the top of the Chrysler Headquarters building for more modest digs beside the engineering offices.

[Mind you, this can be really dicey if you are a Harvard trained manage-by-the-numbers guy, which was pretty much what business schools cranked out for quite a number of years. If you don't know a torque wrench from a battery tester, maybe stay in your office and read management reports, sales projections, and other works of fiction.]

In "The day I met Sergio Marchionne" (CAR, 15 August 2012), Georg Kacher describes Marchionne and his R&D wizard, Ferdinand Piech, as sharing:

> "... a deep understanding of the business they are shaping ...."

Here is a CEO who actually understands the business he is in, and wants to make the business grow.

Green Sticky Note: The business school ideal of the manage-by-the-numbers executive seems to have its limitations. That a CEO should actually understand the business he is in seems to have been lost on many companies. How do we de-emphasize manage-by-the-numbers, and reintroduce as a standard management concept that C-levels need to really understand both the demand side and the supply side of the business?

That finishes my set of sticky notes drawn from observation of the Shill Game. Have you added yours?

We have seen how bad business behaviors driven by stock market and investor consideration can be wasteful, but at least they are "legal". Then, there is the Shell Game. This is where things go from legal, to sort-of legal (if you look at it the "right" way), to outright misrepresentation and fraud. Next up, the Shell Game.

Notes: (Yellow: root cause; Blue: proposed solution; Green: question or additional data we need)

_____

_____

_____

_____

_____

_____

_____

_____

_____

_____

_____

_____

_____

_____

_____

_____

"It is not that humans have become any more greedy than in generations past. It is that the avenues to express greed have grown so enormously." (Alan Greenspan, 2002)

Chapter 10 – The Shell Game

We are all familiar with the Shell Game – the "now you see it, now you don't" parlor trick that proves the hand is faster than the eye. The corporate Shell Game, rather than being simple amusement, is deadly. Practiced with ever increasing skill and cunning, it is deadly to shareholders, and deadly to the country's welfare. It shows that the accountant's math is quicker and more devious than the investor's eye. How interesting that someone called "Skilling" would demonstrate that "skill" to make a "killing" – and take down the markets in the process.

It is also interesting that we actually seem to inherently recognize and even accept the way this game is played. After all, we actually talk about "Shell companies".

The Acquisitions Gambit

There are a number of ways to play the shell game. One is called "Acquisitions". Nortel, who only a few short years ago employed thousands of people in my current hometown and is now essentially bankrupt, was a great example of this brilliant gambit.

The trick to playing this successfully is to make sure that no one is watching both the top line and the bottom line at the same time. It also relies on investors not knowing very much about the clash of cultures that often occurs with corporate mergers.

So the way this game works is this. First, you build a moderate sized real company, with real products and modest revenue. Then you go on an acquisitions binge – get big or get out! Acquiring existing businesses beats having them as competitors.

You buy market share, you buy (hopefully) complementary products, complementary skill sets, and manufacturing resources. You might have an opportunity to, in effect, "corner" the market in your segment.

You also buy the top line revenue of the acquired company. Now on a market chart, this looks really great. Last year your revenue was $200 million. This year your revenue is $400 million. You must be a very sharp businessman. You're worth the "hockey star" salary you are making.

Well, maybe, maybe not. You just added a whack load of debt, or a whack load of extra shareholders, or both. You added a whack load of employees on salary, and machines, work in process, aged inventory, leased space, ….you name it. You also now have to merge two or more cultures, management styles, business processes, and product lines.

Companies who are doing very well on their own don't seem to go on the same kind of super-sized acquisition binges. Yes, they might occasionally see a complementary opportunity, and pursue it to systematically build their business, but that is not my definition of a binge.

My perception is that acquisition binges happen more often with companies that are struggling for consistent bottom line profit. And as a consequence, the results are all too often disaster down the road – as happened with Nortel. By then, of course, many of the C-level execs who played the acquisitions gambit are long gone, having cashed in their chips at the door.

One of the supposed effects of mergers is economy of scale, so maybe you don't need all those facilities and all of those people. Let's "rationalize" our operations. Close some facilities, lay off or buy out some of the workforce. Let's get our cost base down.

Now the stock market has been shown time and again to love this line of thinking. Lay off a bunch of employees. The stock goes up. Close a plant. The stock goes up again.

If you consider that employees actually make the stuff you sell, in the plants that you close, it seems self-evident that you are reducing production capacity – so will have to either put your prices up and chance losing market share or have your revenue go down. If you were losing money before, you can now lose it even faster. And once you start down this road, half of your staff – especially the smart ones, the productive ones – start dusting off their resumes, and sometimes talking to the competition.

Why does the market respond this way? Because the Shills are making money on money, not on production of goods and services!

So just how nutzoid can the acquisition gambit become? Take a look at this list. Tyco Semiconductor started in 1962 in Massachusetts, and went public in 1964. (Source: http://en.wikipedia.org/wiki/Tyco_International)

In the 1970's, Tyco acquired:

- Mule Battery Products
- Simplex Technology
- Grinnell Fire Protection Systems
- Armin Plastics
- The Ludlow Corporation

1980's
- Grinnell Corporation
- Allied Tube and Conduit
- The Mueller Company

In the 1990's, mainly under CEO Dennis Kozlowski:
- Wormald International Limited
- Neotecha
- Hindle/Winn
- Classic Medical
- Uni-Patch
- Promeon
- Preferred Pipe

- Kendall International Co.
- Tectron Tube
- Unistrut
- Earth Technology Corporation
- Professional Medical Products, Inc.
- Thorn Security
- Carlisle
- Watts Waterworks Businesses
- Sempell
- ElectroStar
- American Pipe & Tube
- Submarine Systems Inc.
- Keystone
- INBRAND
- Sherwood Davis & Geck
- United States Surgical
- Wells Fargo Alarm
- AMP
- Raychem
- Glynwed
- Temasa
- Central Sprinkler

Get big or get out! Acquisitions continued into the twenty-first century, but a few things went awry. This included:

1. A downgrade of Tyco's credit rating, which made borrowing more expensive.
2. Losses in the electronics segment - $2 Billion in red ink.
3. Losses and restructuring charges in underwater fiber optics - $3.5 Billion.
4. Electronics restructuring charges, inventory write-downs, and facilities closures - $1 Billion in red ink.
5. Goodwill impairments - $750 Million.
6. Losses in investments - $1 Billion.

That totals over $8 Billion, and was not the end of it, but makes the point. Get really big – **lose** really big.

If all of the 38 companies that Tyco acquired over the years had remained independent operating companies, would the U.S. economy be better off? Tyco's problems were a key factor in kyboshing the recovery of the market after the attack on 9/11.

What drives companies to get so massive, and then lose in spectacular fashion? It can usually be traced to ambition and greed by people at the top. Arrogance at the C-level, and often extending much deeper into middle management, also seems to be a factor.

We have not seen the last of Tyco in this narrative. They reappear in the "Steal Game". Does this come as a surprise? It shouldn't. Greed and theft have common ancestors - the worship of money and the complete absence of morals or concern for anyone but oneself.

The Off-the-Books Gambit

If the Nortel and Tyco examples show the dangers inherent in the Acquisitions Gambit, they are at least legal – if stupid. The Off-the-Books Gambit crosses the line. It is enabled by the same companies-too-big-to-handle issue, but plays out in a totally different way.

And it takes collusion. It takes people who are willing to lie and cheat, and other people who are willing to turn a blind eye to the lying and cheating – including the very people who are supposed to be protecting "we the people" from such abuse.

On September 11, 2001, terrorists attacked the Twin Towers, and not too long after that, America was at war with Iraq. But people whom I consider domestic terrorists – people whose ideology is unadulterated greed – proceeded to do much or more damage to the U.S. economy than the Wahabiist attackers could ever have done. (With 98,000 people dying every year in the U.S. from preventable medical errors, our priorities are totally skewed.)

The 9/11 terrorists were brought up and educated in a restrictive, dogmatic, and hate-filled environment. U.S. born managers and senior executives were brought up in an open, free, and dynamic environment. Many of them have religious affiliations. Yet some of these C-levels callously line their own pocket with zero concern for the fallout – for the damage to the economy and for the broken lives (and deaths) that they leave behind – because what they really worship is money.

Only scant weeks after 9/11, on Oct 1st of 2001, the Enron scandal hit the news. Ultimately, shareholders lost nearly $ 11 Billion. That was the loss directly attributed to Enron, but is the tip of the iceberg when the ripple effect through the markets is factored in.

Enron was a classic Shell Game. President Jeffrey Skilling and CFO Andrew Fastow systematically moved company losses into shell entities to get them off the books, and keep the stock price climbing.

In typical fashion, when things started to get tense, Skilling left the company, and then cashed in on $60 Million in stock options, before the proverbial sh** hit the fan. Ultimately 20,000 employees lost their jobs, and many of them lost their life savings, when their 401K-pension plan lost $1 Billion. Skilling is now serving 24 years in Federal prison.

So how did they get away with it? Wasn't anyone watching? Well, three Merrill Lynch bankers were found guilty of helping inflate Enron's profits, but they were acquitted on appeal. Arthur Anderson consulting, which was one of the five largest audit firms in the world, went down with Enron.

Was Republican Senator Phil Gramm's wife, Wendy, really a directory of Enron? You might remember Gramm from his key role in the Financial Services Modernization Act and the Commodities Futures Modernization Act, both key pieces of legislation that made the Enron debacle possible. Do a little sleuthing on the web and see what you find.

The Sarbanes-Oxley Act directly resulted from the Enron fraud – one of the numerous pieces of legislation that regularly come under fire from the right wing for "over-regulation" of business in the U.S., and which is now costing large companies about $2 – 3 million a year in extra audit fees. Which of course makes me ask: "So exactly what were the auditors doing prior to Sarbanes-Oxley"?

The Enron scandal, together with the 9/11 attacks, resulted in a loss on the U.S Markets of an estimated $7 Trillion. Do you wonder who's pocket that ended up in? How many jobs does that kill? How many lives have been ruined?

About the same time that Skilling and Fastow were working their Shell Game at Enron, Worldcom CEO Bernie Ebbers was busy using Worldcom Stock and corporate loan guarantees to finance his risky bets on the stock market and his other ventures.

Meanwhile, the CFO, Comptroller, and Director of General Accounting were cooking the books to cover up losses and overstate revenues to inflate Worldcom Stock. In 2002, Worldcom filed for bankruptcy protection.

These individual massive cases did untold damage to the U.S. economy, and in fact to the economy of most of America's trading partners. But the real fallout came through game number 3 – Short Selling.

Cracking the Shells' Eggs

Blue Sticky Note: Proposed solution – Put them in jail! That was simple. Well …. Maybe it's a spot more complicated than that. Some of the more outrageous cases have resulted in jail terms, but many who were at least in part responsible got off the hook. But there are other things that could be done to prevent the problems in the first place. Let's break it down a bit.

Yellow Sticky Note: Root problem – Use of acquisition to make the company grow fast.

Blue Sticky Note: Proposed solution – C-level stock-sale freeze for three years after leaving a company, and penalty clauses in management compensation agreement.

Green Sticky Note: If a company goes rapidly down hill when a C-level leaves, is that an indicator that the CEO was really, really good, or really, really bad? How could we find out?

My Notes for the Team Meeting: Depending on the circumstances, penalty clauses in management agreements could include options/salary/bonus claw-back if the CEO buys a lemon, or if balance sheet, cultural, or structural issues show up after the fact, demonstrating that acquisitions were a "dumb or dumber" move, or that oversight of the finances was sloppy at best.

Unfair? Look, these guys make the big bucks because they are smart, they understand the business, they know how to make money, they know how to make the business grow. They also are eying the market opportunities, and have figured out the strategic acquisitions that will position the company for new opportunities going forward. Fair.

Monologue: *"Yes, the Board of Directors is issuing a formal request that you return your $18 Million in salary and $6 Million in bonuses from last year. Yes. Well we realize it might take a week or two, especially to get it from your Cayman's account."*

"You should be able to get a fair bit back to live on from the tax department. Oh, really? You didn't pay much in taxes? We need to get to know your tax accountant."

"How will you explain it to your wife? That you screwed up? Oh? She thinks you're brilliant? Of course. Well if you could convince her of that, I'm sure you'll think of something. Perhaps you could make her feel better by taking her to the opera. Pardon? No! You can't put that on our expense account."

"Well, we did look at other options, but in truth some of the shareholders and staff seriously wanted to take a chunk right out of your hide."

"We managed to calm them down a bit. They have taken their letter openers and piano wire back to their offices. We can probably keep them at bay ... if you can have the money back in thirty days."

If the CEO had been operating under these rules of engagement, would Nortel have gone on an acquisition binge that was a major factor in destroying the company, costing investors and pensioners big time, to say nothing of losing all those patents to foreign companies? Not bloody likely.

No, he would have been more cautious, because he would have had skin in the game. But under the current rules he could be the high roller, the wonder wiz that took the company to new heights in revenue never seen before, and who could then cash out his chips, bank his salary, and walk away from the mess. "My room is dirty? Let the servants clean it up. I'm going to the movies."

Yellow Sticky Note: Root problem – Cooking the books.

Blue Sticky Note: Proposed solution – There should be restitution, with costs, for all consequence of such actions – not out of government coffers, but directly out of the cook's (or cooks' – 'cause there is generally collusion) bank accounts – offshore or onshore – and/or through seizure and sale of assets. Oh yes, and jail terms.

That finishes my set of sticky notes drawn from observation of the Shell Game. Have you added yours? Next up, the Short Game.

Notes: (Yellow: root cause; Blue: proposed solution; Green: question or additional data we need)

"He didn't raise interest rates to curb the market's enthusiasm; he didn't even seek to impose margin requirements on stock market investors. Instead, he waited until the bubble burst, as it did in 2000, then tried to clean up the mess afterward."
(Nobel laureate Paul Krugman, writing about Alan Greenspan)

Chapter 11 – The Short Game

I have a bridge for sale – in Brooklyn. Do you believe that? Probably not! But, if I could sell it, and make a profit, and the New York City Department of Transport found out, I would be in deep doo-doo. I would end up in jail for fraud – for selling something that did not belong to me.

Now in golf, the short game is the well-understood difference between the Pro Tour and the rest of us. In the securities market, the short game is a big chunk of the difference between the 0.001 percent who collectively own $19 trillion dollars, and the rest of us who range from struggling to reasonably well off.

Shorting stocks has been around essentially since the early days of the stock markets. In 1609, Isaac le Maire and eight other people founded a secret company, the so-called "Grote Compagnie", with the primary purpose to trade in the shares of the Vereenigde Oostindische Compagnie (VOC, or Dutch East India Company for those of you whose Dutch is a spot rusty).

Le Maire had a deep resentment of VOC, having been forced out from the high position of governor of the company over some little matters of expenses and receipts that is largely shrouded in mystery, but perhaps is indicative of character. A part of the settlement included waiving any rights to become a competitor to VOC. He subsequently conspired with both the French and the British in an attempt to outmaneuver his former enterprise.

But he also still held nearly one quarter of the VOC shares. Le Maire's plan seemed simple. He and his business partners "shorted" the VOC stock – that is, they sold large numbers of shares on the market, shares that they did not actually own. Now dumping large numbers of shares on the market in a short time always causes a depression of the share price. The old supply and demand thing kicks in.

They then spread rumors that caused the stock price to go down even farther. The idea was to get the price down low enough that they could then buy back a sufficient number of shares to cover what they had sold (but did not own). Of course this hurt all of the shareholders of VOC, but so what? That was undoubtedly a big part of Le Maire's motive.

Unfortunately for him and his fellow conspirators, in 1610 the government brought in regulations making it illegal to sell shares that are not in one's possession. "Ya don't own the Brooklyn Bridge, so y'all can't sell it." What a concept.

Now Le Maire argued that the restriction was unnecessary, and the drop in share price was really because of bad business practices at VOC. Do you hear an echo in the room?

Once the regulation was brought in, however, and in spite of VOC's supposedly bad business practices, the stock price had doubled by 1611, and members of Le Maire's gang had to cover their position at higher prices.

Several of them went bankrupt. Le Maire himself lost money, but was able to extricate himself while still solvent. He went on scheming, and for your amusement and edification, you can find lots about his further adventures and misadventures on Wikipedia.

Just Try to Fix It

If we were collectively smart, that would have been the beginning and the end of short selling. No such luck. The Dutch made it illegal in 1610. The British banned "naked short selling" in 1733. In the Republic of France, Napoleon Bonaparte outlawed short selling, and had short sellers imprisoned as treasonous and unpatriotic.

In the U.S., it was banned after speculation during the War of 1812. This legislation was repealed in the wild-west days of the 1850's, and then restricted again in 1938 (but not outlawed) after the crash in 1929 and the Great Depression that followed. During the '29 crash, one short-seller, trader Jesse Livermore pocketed over $100 million selling stuff he didn't really own. Imagine how much that is adjusted for inflation to 2012 dollars!

But in spite of the frequent attempts to stop or reign in the practice, it keeps coming back – like the bad smell from a garbage dump. And every time, it causes a lot of ordinary folk to lose a lot of money. "Why?" you might ask. 'Cause it makes a lot of people a little money, and a few people a LOT of money. And people making some money say, "gee, that's ok" and those who stand to make lots of money – they just pressure (or outright buy) the lawmakers.

Well It Must Be O.K., Isn't It?

Scratch anyone in the brokerage business, and they will tell you that short selling bans have been repealed because:

"… short sellers have a significant role in the markets."

(http://www.investopedia.com/articles/stocks/09/short-selling-ban.asp#axzz28dDB4v1p0)

Well, yes they do have a "significant role". I'll agree with that. But is it a positive role? What does Investopedia say about that?

According to Investopedia, the Securities Exchange Commission (SEC) identifies the importance of short-sellers based on their:

- Contribution to efficient price discovery
- Mitigating market bubbles
- Increasing market liquidity
- Promotion of capital formation
- Facilitating hedging and other management activities
- Limits to upward market manipulation"

Investopedia goes on to explain how short seller James Chanos examined Enron's accounting practices and discovered that something was amiss, ultimately putting some of the Enron executives behind bars.

You just gotta admit this sounds pretty good, right? Bless their little gold-plated short-selling hearts!

In the various principles and practices associated with Lean Manufacturing is something called root-cause analysis, and the five Why's. The principle says if you want to fix something that is broken, you need to trace the problem back to the source, and fix the problem "at source".

You must never put band-aids over the bleeding and ignore the source of the problem. You might have to ask a whole series of "Why" questions, to really figure out what the root of the problem is. This must be a totally foreign notion to the folks in the securities biz, and in government.

But let's just play the "root cause game" with each of the listed reasons for the important role of short selling. I'll lead you through the first in detail, and then more quickly summarize the process for the others,

The first is "contribution to efficient price discovery". Price discovery is a process that establishes the true value of an asset. So to play the game, let's ask:

1. "Why don't we know the real value of the asset?" (… in this case, the true value of shares in Company A)
"Because buyers have been bidding it up over its true value."

2. "Why would they do that – why would they pay more than it is worth?"
"Because they think it is worth more than it is."

3. "Why would they think it is worth more than it is?"
"Because their broker told them it was a great buy."

4. "Why would their broker tell them that, if it is not true?"

Now there are two possible answers to this – the Shill Game, and the Shell Game – neither having anything to do with short selling.

So rather than suggesting we depend on short sellers like James Chanos to discover that Enron is a house of cards (Shell Game) – and accepting that he will coincidently get very, very rich in the process, while wiping out peoples' 401Ks and leaving them in the streets – how about fixing the root problem(s)?

In the interests of brevity, I am going to gang "Mitigating market bubbles" and "Limits to upward market manipulation" together, because like "price discovery", a certain pattern sets in – very quickly.

In fact, by simply replacing the word "asset" in the first "why" question with "market", and following though, we come down to the root cause of market bubbles – the Shill Game. Market bubbles happen because of the direct actions of brokers – who know they win when the markets go up, and they win when the markets go down.

In the case of limiting upward market manipulation, "manipulation" says it all. Now there is a direct answer to question 4. Their broker did not tell them because he did not know that the C-levels were cooking the books!

Yet the brokerage firms (presumably) had the same information available to them that James Chanos did – unless of course Chanos had someone inside Enron go "psssst" in his ear. With the amount of money Chanos stood to make, one cannot rule this out.

Certainly people at Merrill Lynch knew what was going on. So did the people at Arthur Anderson. They were the people morally and legally obligated to prevent the manipulation. If they had gone public much earlier, at the risk of losing some crooked C-level folks as customers, much of Enron might have survived, and with it the jobs and 401Ks of literally thousands of people, to say nothing of the massive other losses the Enron scandal triggered.

The root cause of upward market manipulation is the conspiracy of banks, brokerage firms, audit firms, accountants and C-level executives. Fix that, and you don't need short sellers to mitigate and limit.

So let's look at the next great roll for the short seller – "Facilitating hedging and other management activities". Now there is a word missing here, and that is the word "risk" before "management activities". "Management activities" has a sort of neutral to positive ring about it. "Risk management", on the other hand, suggests gambling – which is precisely what hedging is about. It sounds like such a good thing when it rolls off the tongue of the Shills. Hedging depends on being able to sell short, to sell something you don't own, and short selling "has an important role" because it "facilitates hedging". Does something about that sound like a circular argument? Give me a break!

Now I have left the last two "roles" – "increasing market liquidity" and "promotion of capital formation" until last, mainly because they are such incredibly good examples of what George Orwell, in his famous utopian horror story Nineteen Eighty-Four, called doublethink. (Here is a really interesting piece of trivia – Orwell's book came out in 1949, the same year that Alfred Winslow Jones started the first hedge fund.)

Liquidity is a good thing, right? Liquidity means that if I own a stock, and I want to sell it, that I am able to find a buyer for it at a reasonable agreed price. Such stock is considered a "liquid" asset. But if I have a stock, and absolutely no one wants it, that stock would be considered "non-liquid" or worthless.

So exactly how does a short seller increase market liquidity? He doesn't. He increases market volume, because he dumps more stock on the market than there are buyers at that price point, so the stock goes down. What does that do for my stock? It makes it harder for me to find a buyer at a reasonable agreed price, because so many shares have been dumped on the market. We have anti-dumping policies for trade goods – but not for shares. So from my vantage point, short selling decreases market liquidity. Unless you follow the Party newspeak – words like "blackwhite" and "liquidfrozen".

And finally there is "capital formation". But in order for someone to short sell stock, the company must already be capitalized, or there IS no stock to sell. So exactly how can trading stocks through short selling create or form new capital. Obviously it can't. It can create a large "new" pool of capital by taking old capital out of my hands and giving it to new owners – all done without my permission. This is not formation of anything. It is simply legalized theft.

So explain to me again why short selling provides any positive value to the market whatsoever? … without using newspeak, or requiring that all the history of perversion of the markets by greedy leeches be dumped into the "memory hole".

Do you still believe that short sellers have a significant (positive) role in the marketplace? If you do, as I said at the beginning of this chapter, I have a bridge for sale.

Why Brokers Like Short Selling

So short selling can make really big money for a few people. But why would brokers want to buy into this? Two very simple reasons:

First, short selling in already volatile markets triggers even more volatility. And every buy-sell order is a little money in the broker's pocket.

But there is another reason. "Naked" short selling is still prohibited in most jurisdictions. That doesn't mean it does not happen, but it is breaking the law in many countries. Naked short selling means that the short seller does not have the stock in hand that he is selling, nor any guaranteed way of getting his hands on the shares.

But to get rich quick, short selling is the best game in stock-market land, so the market establishment had to find a way around the naked short restriction. The solution they came up with was simple. The short seller just "borrows" the shares he needs, sell them at the current market price, and then when the bottom falls out of the market and the share price is much lower, buys them back at the lower price, and returns them to the lender, pocketing the difference.

Would you loan your car to a stranger, let him joy-ride it around town, side-swiping parked cars, running red lights, flying over speed bumps, and then thank him when he brought the remains back to you? Probably not! So why would you loan a stranger your stock, knowing full well that he intended to use it to drive down the price, and give it back to you just as battered as that car? The simple answer is, you wouldn't.

But you don't usually have a say in it. That's the beauty of the system. Check your brokerage statements. Look for the words "unsegregated". That means you own shares of a given stock, but those shares are just a small part of a huge pool of shares from hundreds or even thousands of individual small investors like you.

So when the short seller wants to joy ride your stock into oblivion, he borrows from the pool. Isn't that nice? He doesn't have to bother you with the details. He just borrows the shares he needs from the broker holding that pool, and he is in business.

The broker is happy to oblige, because the broker charges fees and/or gets interest on the loan. So the broker loves to talk to short sellers. He makes his fee or interest, and then he makes commissions on sales resulting from the volatility. This is a double win for the broker, and he really doesn't care which way the stock price goes.

If you are a big player in the market, your shares might be segregated, so you play by a different set of rules. Now the broker needs your permission to loan the shares, and you might get a part of the proceeds. You would take up such a deal only if you figured the short-seller would get caught by the market actually going up – which does happen sometimes.

If you are a small player, like me, you don't even know the short selling is going on, and you get squat for the loan, and junk shares at the end of the ride.

So the next time you hear a broker defending the "value" in the market of short selling, remind him that the value he is talking about is for him – not for you.

On Train Wrecks and Avalanches

We've been skirting around the big issue associated with shorting stocks in the market. We know that this practice has had a role in serious recessions and in market crashes, and that after serious crashes, legislation has been used to lock the barn door after the horse was out, or perhaps more precisely – after the horse was stolen.

Up here in the great frozen North, wintertime in the mountains can bring with it some hazards – one of which is avalanches. Slippery slopes are rather fun when you have skis strapped to your feet, and good company, a glass of Glühwein, and a hot-tub waiting at the end of the day. But if the slippery slope is unstable, it can come crashing down in a matter of seconds, snapping trees like matchsticks, carrying massive boulders, and devastating anything in its path.

So in the ski resorts of the Rockies, professional mountaineers monitor the snow conditions constantly, and even use explosive devices to trigger small controlled slides before dangerous conditions arise.

But there are a lot of mountains out there, and we can't always watch them all, and people do get killed nearly every year. Back in 1910, an avalanche in the Cascade Mountains actually engulfed two trains of the Great Northern Railway, and 98 people died. Several factors had set up the conditions over time, including timber clear-cutting, a forest fire that was triggered by sparks from the coal-fired engines passing through the area, and at the immediate time of the avalanche, a heavy rain and thunderstorms.

A market crash is pretty much the same as an avalanche, and also results from multiple factors set up over time, which are typically triggered by a storm. Perfectly functional and profitable companies are swept off the tracks to tumble into the abyss. The economy is one colossal train wreck. And some people die, while others are badly injured.

And the professionals in the government and in the financial sector that should have been watching the avalanche conditions were instead drinking Glühwein in the hot tub, and ogling the babes. "What conditions?" you might ask.

In Chapter 7 we mentioned "sell stops", and how they are used by investors to limit their loses in the event that a stock falls below a certain price. The sell stop is triggered automatically, dumping the investor's shares at the current market price, before the price goes too much lower.

But if the investor is buying on margin – that is, is running a chunk of his investing by borrowing funds for further stock purchases against the value of the stocks he already holds, we have the start of a slippery slope. This is a very common practice, almost universally used by big investors. How does this work?

Well suppose I could buy 1000 shares of stock X for $1 a share. If I pay cash, and then sell the stock when it hits $2, I make 100% profit on my original investment. But if I could borrow $500 from the broker, with other stock that I hold as collateral for the loan, I now only need $500 in cash together with the loan to by my 1000 shares, and after I pay back the loan I have made a 200% profit on my original $500. Sweet deal!

The catch in this is that the collateral for the loan is not something solid and stable like the kind of collateral a bank manager wants. Rather, it is other stocks, whose value can be going up or down at any time. If my other stocks are going up, that gives me more margin to play with, which lets me buy more stocks, and if those also go up, then I have more margin … and Wow! Those dot coms I have are roaring, and I am making money hand over fist.

Could this kind of investing create a market bubble? You betcha. Which is why Paul Krugman, among others, criticized Alan Greenspan of the Fed for not tightening margin requirements in the 1990s.

Now being a prudent investor, I don't have all of my stocks in dot coms. I have some in nice solid manufacturing companies, like Nortel and Lucent and Tyco – benefiting from the dot.com build-out, but with track records, and traditional business models – maybe some mining stocks, blue chips that pay dividends, you name it. And I have everything covered with sell-stops, so I can't lose big. Right?

Now take this investor, and his strategy, and multiply by the 3 Million households that were involved in on-line trading in the year 2000. You have the conditions. Mix in some volatility, add three cups of shell games, blend with some rumors, some negative-market talk, and then add shorting. The sharks are circling. The recipe is right.

Time to trigger the avalanche! Pick a reasonably volatile and somewhat "iffy" stock, and short it – big time. No playing around. Take it down! Use the Internet to get the rumors out.

The shorted target stock falls sharply. In fact, the price falls though a few folks "sell stop" price. That dumps even more shares on the market. Buyers retreat. The price barrels downward. Smelling blood, the sharks move in - more shorting. More sell stops triggered. This stock is toast, and the short sellers have run off with the butter.

But this just gets the snowball rolling downhill. For a real avalanche to occur, we need more involvement. That is supplied by the margin accounts.

(Ring!) *"Hey, Joe. Yeah, it's Sam over at Fidelity. Look, seems what with that big drop in Worldcom yesterday, your margin account is running light. You need to cover 6 grand. Yeah, 6 grand is the number. Yah haven't got the cash right now? Oh!*

"Well you have that Nortel stock that's trading around $100 bucks. I could dump enough shares to cover the 6 G's. O.K. I'll do that for ya."

The collateral damage has started. The avalanche is picking up momentum.

(Click!) *"... and now, in Market News, Nortel dropped sharply below its' thirty and sixty day moving averages. Technical traders see that as a sign that the short-lived rally is over, and the sell-off is picking up steam..."*

(Click!) *"Now the market news for Today. The tech-heavy Nasdaq tumbled 286 points today, dropping below 4000 – the heaviest loss for the exchange since 1987...."*

Between 1999 and 2002, the U.S. equity markets lost $7.6 Trillion – the greatest wealth decline in American history according to John Schroy on the "Capital Flow Analysis" web site. So with this wealth "decline", I wonder where they made the big bonfire to burn all of those thousand-dollar bills?

But of course by then, we had a war in Iraq to worry about, so who had time to figure out what went wrong, or where all that money disappeared to?

Cracking the Shorts' Eggs

Yellow Sticky Note: Root problem – Shorting stock, a.k.a selling something you don't own, a.k.a legalized theft.

Blue Sticky Note: Proposed solution – Ban it, and keep it banned, from all markets – for all time.

My Notes for the Team Meeting: Short selling clearly has none of the beneficial functions attributed to it, makes fortunes for the destroyers, and encourages negative behavior. The supposed "benefits" are doublespeak - all smoke and mirrors. If we adopt pay-for-performance so that brokers are now paid to make us money, they no longer really benefit from shorting either. In fact, they could lose perfectly good commissions on profits. Come to think of it, once brokers are on pay-for-performance instead of pay-per-trade, the brokers (who currently defend the practice and the players) might tear short sellers limb from limb.

Notes: (Yellow: root cause; Blue: proposed solution; Green: question or additional data we need)

_____

_____

_____

"SMITHERS—(with curiosity) And I bet you got yer pile o' money 'id safe some place.

"JONES—(with satisfaction) I sho' has! And it's in a foreign bank where no pusson don't ever git it out but me no matter what come. You didn't s'pose I was holdin' down dis Emperor job for de glory in it, did you?"

(Eugene O'Neill –The Emperor Jones, 1920)

Chapter 12 – The Steal Game

In baseball, the art of stealing is a highly regarded and very useful skill set for players to develop. Watch for the pitcher to take his eye off you, and commit himself – then run like hell. Stealing is not usually so well regarded in business, or in government, but a lot of it goes on. Every once in a blue moon someone gets caught, but these occasions are likely just the tip of the iceberg.

The Hand in the Cookie Jar Gambit

Now there are many different variations of the steal game in business. One is just simple theft. Wait until no one is looking, and then take the money and run, or hide in plain sight and cover up the evidence. At the low end, stealing might be petty theft, like cheating on expense accounts. You'll recall that Le Maire was turfed from his position as governor of the Dutch East India Company, apparently for shenanigans with expenses. A crook is a crook – it is not a matter of degree.

Remember I said we would return to Tyco. I don't forget Tyco, because shenanigans there cost my small company a $40,000 contract.

It happened like this. We had a training package that their electronics-manufacturing arm needed, and wanted. We were introduced by a dealer in Massachusetts who knew their needs and had the contacts.

We headed down to meet with their team, and the guy inside Tyco with the problem – and the budget – introduced the meeting by explaining to his team all of the reasons that our solution made perfect sense for them. Needless to say we agreed with him, got along famously, and left it to our dealer to get a quote ready.

The dealer did so, but did not get it to the decision maker for his signature until late on Friday. By Monday, said decision maker was on a two-week holiday, so the P.O was on hold until he returned. By the time that decision maker got back, all hell had broken loose, Tyco's stock price was falling like a stone, layoffs were looming, and our virtually "certain" $40,000 deal was dead in the water, part of the ripple effect that accompanies all of these games.

So what happened? Well it was quite complex, but in a nutshell, the CEO and CFO were caught with their hands in the cookie jar. Look up Tyco stock scandal on the web. It is all there, including the stock fraud, the $6000 shower curtains, and the $2 Million dollar birthday party that CEO Kozlowski threw for his wife at a resort in Sardinia, half of it paid for by Tyco.

In the end game, a jury found former CEO Kozlowski and CFO Swartz guilty of stealing $150 Million from Tyco, and they were sentenced to a minimum of eight and one-third years in prison. Fortunately, although it helped thoroughly mess up the market in 2002, this game did not take Tyco itself down permanently. In that way, it was not another Enron.

What causes people to behave like this? What is their thinking? I was once an unwitting dupe in a sort-of shell game/steal game, that in the end caused me to break up an early business partnership.

So how did this one go? Well, we had two fairly distinct lines of business. I started the first with said business partner – developing interactive computer-based training and interactive trade-show and museum exhibits.

We were moderately successful, and our activities attracted a third partner to a new line of business – building an interactive business directory for the World's largest shopping mall.

Our two businesses operated in a symbiotic fashion for a time, but there were some small conflicts over resources that lead to a spatial separation into adjacent offices, a clearer division of roles, but also some wasteful (in my mind) duplication of services.

At year end, when I looked at the books of both companies, low and behold I discovered that my original partner had paid himself twice – once from company A with my co-signature, and once from company B with the other partner's co-signature.

I guess he figured no one would bother to check. When confronted with this obvious breach of trust, and asked why he did it, he had a four-word answer: "I needed the money". We parted company and split out the business ownership, with he and his other partner going their own way.

In his mind, he was perfectly justified in ripping me off. He obviously did not see it as stealing. He was a nice guy, a bright guy, but apparently had a deep down sense of "entitlement". I think this sense of entitlement accounts for most bad behavior by business people.

Cracking the Stolen Eggs

Yellow Sticky Note: Root problem – Crooks at the C-level, who have an "entitlement" gene.

Blue Sticky Note: Proposed solution – In serious cases, put them in jail when you catch them, and get full restitution with costs. And don't treat them like some kind of celebrity.

Monologue: *"Tapeworm, meet your new cellmate, roundworm. That's maggot and slug in the next cell. You sit with them at suppertime. I am sure you will find you have a lot in common"*

Monologue: *"Sorry Bimbo. Those rocks belong to the state now, along with your pink Lamborghini, 35-bedroom house with the 3 swimming pools and 7-car garage. We are turning it into a seniors' home for some of the pensioners who lost money on your hubby's scam.*

Green Sticky Note: How can we improve the oversight of company assets to catch this kind of thing earlier?

Yellow Sticky Note: Root problem – Monitoring accounts and tracking funds.

Blue Sticky Note: Proposed solution – Improve accounting oversight, and dismember any accounting firm with three or more auditors who collude with clients to cook the books. Put both the accountants and their clients in jail.

Green Sticky Note: How is it that today's high speed intelligent monitoring systems can pick up a fraudulent transaction on my credit card, and call me within minutes to confirm, but Enron can salt away millions of dollars in fraudulent transactions and not be caught for four years? Does this mystify you like it mystifies me?

The Insider Trading Gambit

So there is straight outright theft or breach of trust. Then there is a slight variation on the Short Game, but with stocks you actually own. It is called "insider trading".

Insider trading involves the quick sale of shares on the open market by people with inside knowledge that something not very nice is about to become public, and something that will probably knock the stock price down.

"Pssssst! The CEO has had his hand in the cookie jar. Looks like the broadsheet will hit the fan anytime. Sell now, sell it all, before the bottom falls out."

Now the insider might be the owner of the stock, usually a C-level exec who actually knows how much money they lost last quarter, or might be a friend or relative, or even a broker who has come by what is supposed to be confidential information.

Maybe it is not a hand in the cookie jar. Maybe it's other bad news, like "our cancer drug is not getting the expected FDA approval after all". You can ask Martha Stewart about that kind of thing. She probably has a better understanding of the consequences now than she did in 2002.

And in all fairness to Stewart, she was a pretty small fish in this whole thing, and probably somewhat naïve – and consequently served a very short sentence. But she was a big fish in other ponds, so took a lot more heat than many other non-celebrities would have in similar circumstances.

But virtually every time a company goes down, including Tyco, Nortel, Enron, and WorldCom, some C-level execs or ex-execs have been caught in insider trades. The temptation is just too great, and it seems to be pretty easy for many of these folks to justify in their own mind that they are not **really** doing anything wrong. Their moral compass is just a shade off true North. They are entitled.

The Shell Game Gambit

Yet another Steal Game is a variation of the Shell Game – move money or assets to a different shell company, and then appropriate it from there. This hollowing out of companies is an easy way to screw shareholders, and used with regularity. A variant involves selling all or part of the company, and messing with the shares during the transfer. I have stock now worth effectively 0.001 cents a share, down from around $3.10 a share when I initially purchased it, in a company that is still operating, still making a profit, but has changed ownership at least 3 times.

Banker's Punto Banco (with a stacked deck)

But all of these previous thefts together don't even start to come close to the magnitude of theft that occurs inside banks – taking huge bites out of the economy, out of middle class wealth, and out of tax revenue through bailouts. Yes, banks and educated fleas do it – and I mean suck the lifeblood – not fall in love. There are two prominent gambits here

The Rogue Trading Gambit

Nick Leeson brought down Barings Bank, the oldest investment bank in the U.K. Some sources suggest that he was denied a broker's license in the UK because of fraud on his license application. If so, this should have been a leading-indicator of where things would go. Character flaws and an entitlement complex show up early if you are looking for them.

But rather than shooing him out the door, in 1992 Barings appointed him general manager of their futures trading operations in Singapore, where he started a pattern of unauthorized and highly speculative trades. Furthermore, he was not subject to certain oversights that were common in the industry.

He got lucky in early trades, earning large commissions for his contribution to Barings' profits.

Then things started to sour, and he played a shell game with error accounts to hide his growing losses. This continued for over two years. When his last desperate attempt to recoup his losses failed, he fled Singapore.

By the time the dust settled, losses for Barings totaled about $1.4 Billion. After a failed bailout attempt, Barings was declared insolvent – with all of the fallout in the market and costs to taxpayers that a bank failure entails. Leeson was eventually tracked down, arrested, and spent the next few years behind bars in Singapore.

He was not the first, and probably not the last to attempt the rogue-trading gambit, for personal or company profit.

Yellow Sticky Note: Root problem – Hiring crooks.

Blue Sticky Note: Proposed solution – Screen them out early. In Lean, this is called "mistake proofing".

Green Sticky Note: Are there some personality tests, and tracking procedures that would be appropriate for C-Level execs and others in positions of responsibility and authority that could help?

My Notes for the Team Meeting: Look at what happened with Barring's Bank. They knew Leeson had cheated to try to get his broker's license. But they put him in charge. With no oversight? Brilliant. Companies submit the janitor to all kinds of tests, from peeing in a bottle to criminal record checks. Are we as diligent with execs?

HR and hiring is not my space so the I really don't know what might actually work, but the Worm Monologs below are my fun look at a real problem.

Monologue: *"Oh. You have a newly minted MBA from an Ivy League college? Step right in. What job would you like, sir? A private stall in the underground lot for your Ferrari? Yeah, should be able to arrange that. An escape chute so you can leave without passing security? Well, we'll have to check with our architect, but I expect we can work something out."*

Monologue: *"So this is called a Rorschach test. I'll show you an inkblot pattern, and you just tell me your first impression of what it is. Don't stress over it. Just whatever pops into your head. Ready? Ok, here we go."*

"What do you think this blob looks like? Money? Ok. And this one? Money again? And this one? A big pile of Money! And this one? Customers and investors leaning over with their backside to you? {Well that's different.} And this one? Gold bars in a Swiss Bank. Good answers! Would you like to be CFO?"

The Slice It Dice It Gambit

When the Republican sponsored CFMA bill was signed into Law in the dying days of the Clinton era, the stage was set for what Les Leopold has rightly called: <u>The Looting of America</u>. This was the culmination of a long period of gradual erosion of Glass-Steagall – the post-depression regulatory Act brought in by the Roosevelt Administration in 1933, which, among other things, prevented lending banks from also being involved in the speculative investment banking area.

A key player in the erosion of the public protection provided by the Glass-Steagall Act bill was the Federal Reserve System, and the process of erosion seems to have started back in 1987.

The Fed is a legal banking cartel with quasi public as well as private banks as members, but with an appointed board of governors and chaired by a Presidential appointee. The Fed structure is, in itself, a bit of a shell game, leading most Americans and much of the rest of the World to believe that the Fed is a government agency and it directly implements Government policy. That's not how it works. It works as a banking cartel.

Established in 1913 by an act of Congress, it has the authority to act independently of the President and the legislative arm, although its activities are "reviewed" by Congress on a periodic basis. I am not going to pretend I really know how this works, or even is supposed to work. I'm not sure that many politicians in Congress "really" know how all this works.

There have been tens of thousands of pages written on the Fed, suggesting it is everything from the greatest triumph of fiscal invention to create world prosperity through to a huge criminal conspiracy, to everything in between. These essentially moral and ethical questions I will leave to be solved by others. But from the straight analytical perspective of its functioning in the value chain, there are some ways to tell when it is not working!

According to Investopedia, the Fed's mandate is:

> "… to promote sustainable growth, high levels of employment, stability of prices to help preserve the purchasing power of the dollar and moderate long-term interest rates."

Does that sound like a description of what has happened since 1987? No, I don't think so either. Maybe what we need to do to prevent cognitive dissonance is to rewrite the charter this way:

> "… to promote two **un**sustainable bubbles, (first in dot.com and then in housing), high levels of **un**employment (third highest in U.S. history by my rough calculation), to promote rapidly rising prices in fundamental needs like health care, food, and energy, to erode purchasing power while the dollar moves into uncharted territory, and to promote long-term interest rates and government debt that puts social security, pension funds, and bond holders at risk."

There. That solves the cognitive dissonance problem. And with this rewritten mandate, perhaps we should also change the name to the **Un**-Fed, since there are a lot of folks out there who are going unfed as a result of their actions – and it could get worse.

The chairman of the Fed though this period of deregulation – starting in with his ascension in 1987 and leading to the CFMA in 2000, and extending to the sub-prime mortgage crisis in 2006 – was one Alan Greenspan.

A household name throughout the Western World, he served for an unprecedented five Presidential terms, three Republican terms under Regan, Bush Senior, and Bush Junior, and two Democrat terms under Clinton.

He has been described as the "rock star" of the financial world. And he, more than any other single person, should be held responsible for the looting of America – not because he did it, but because he enabled it, and completely failed to stop it.

Why did he do so? Primarily because of a strongly held belief system based on the principle that "greed" is good, that greed "holds up the world", that greed ultimately makes everyone prosperous – a philosophy acquired as a founding member of the "Objectivist Movement".

Greenspan was a 24-year-old acolyte of Ayn Rand (the author of Atlas Shrugged) and her out-of-wedlock lover, Nathaniel Branden. An avowed atheist, Ayn Rand was an interesting author with an important story to tell, but she turned into a lousy philosopher with a very limiting worldview, and the arrogance that so often goes with a limited worldview.

It turns out that Greenspan was actually right that greed "holds up" the world. It's just that the methods are more Jesse-James than Henry Ford. Les Leopold eloquently describes the modus operandi for this criminal gang of sub-prime crap shooters in his 200+ page heavily referenced book – The Looting of America – a book that should be mandatory reading for every student of economics and finance, and for every Libertarian in the world.

Many of Leopold's revelations are corroborated by a series of videos made with Catherine Austin Fitts, who was Assistant Secretary of Housing under George H.W. Bush – definitely someone who should have a deep understanding of what has been happening. And Fitts also titles some of her videos "The Looting of America".

What Leopold calls "fantasy finance", Fitts describes – perhaps even more graphically – as the "Tapeworm Economy." So some of the richest people in the world are actually tapeworms. Yes, that is pretty descriptive.

Now I need to be careful here not to leave the impression that I think everyone who has a lot of money is a tapeworm, because that simply is not true. But there are a lot more of them out there than is healthy, and they pretty much know who they are, even if they don't admit it to themselves or anyone else.

So how did the "slice it dice it gambit" work? Well, with the restrictions of Glass-Steagall finally out of the way, the banks and mortgage brokers mixed up a toxic stew by first shilling mortgages to people with modest to marginal capability to service the mortgage debt.

Then, through a slicing/dicing process, the banks produced a series of derivatives products called Collateral Debt Obligations or CDOs. These they sold to unsuspecting organizations like other banks, pension funds, school boards, and hospitals – anyone they could fool into thinking these were safe investments.

Was this illegal? Well, that seems to depend on whom you ask. CDOs were described by Barclay's bank in a 2002 document as "… motivated by the issuing institutions' desire to remove loans and other assets from their balance sheets, to reduce their regulatory capital requirements and improve their return on risk capital." Does that sound like a shell game to you? It does to me as well.

The effect of selling off these CDOs was to return the capital to the bank, thus allowing them to finance yet more mortgages. Since they were passing the risk on existing mortgages to someone else, the normal cautionary behavior of traditional banking went out the window.

This was basically a license to print money. All they had to do was keep the flow of mortgages coming in, slice and dice into CDOs, and sell these off to unsuspecting victims who believed these were safe investments. As Kurt Eggert of the Chapman University School of Law put it:

> "At each stage of the loan and securitization process, securitization encouraged market participants to push risk to the very edge of what the applicable market standards would tolerate, to make the largest, riskiest loans that could be sold on Wall Street, to bundle them using the fewest credit enhancements rating agencies would permit, and then to repeat the securitization process with many of the lower-rated mortgage-backed securities that resulted."

> ("The Great Collapse: How Securitization Caused the Sub prime Meltdown", Kurt Eggert, Chapman University School of Law, May 2009, Connecticut Law Review, Vol. 41, No. 4, 2009.)

So was born the sub-prime mortgage collapse of 2008.

Eggert went on to note:

> "Securitization also created a business model for sub prime lenders whereby they could 'profitably fail.' Thinly capitalized sub prime lenders could generate large numbers of loans likely to default, along with substantial profits for the executives who directed them, and then simply exit the market when they predictably lost their access to the securitization pipeline.

Scoop up the cash, and leave someone else holding the bag.

Now I knew instinctively when the problems first hit that this was not pretty, and that the right wing media spin was exactly that, Spin with a capital "S". But I did not know how bad it really was. Having read Leopold from cover to cover, I now know – and almost wish I didn't. It is hard for me to get into my head that there are so many people out there who "…need the money" and have no problem justifying in their own skull that they are somehow entitled to it (and if that inconveniences a few million other people – well tough!)

Entitlement thinking is always the same. It is just the scale of things that changes. At the low end, a person might have small debts, possibly related to alimony, or gambling loses, or a new wife – that kind of thing.

At the high end, the needs of the multi-billionaires run to things like larger yachts, private jets, trophy brides, building the biggest house in the world (modeled after Versailles) – just the simple pleasures we all should have, and could easily have if we just worked as hard (or smart) as they do. The penultimate American Dream. Keeping up with the Jones's, who just happen to also be multi-billionaires listed on Forbes.com.

But I can't do justice here, in a couple of pages, to what Leopold explained very effectively in 200 pages. So lets just look at a final result of what he called "fantasy finance".

Let's start with the **right wing media Spin** – which in 2008 seemed largely about *those undeserving and nasty people who took out sub-prime mortgages to house their families. Being lazy, uneducated, and feeling "entitled", they were dumb enough to believe the mortgage broker (caveat emptor), and to believe that house prices would continue to rise, increasing their equity* [as housing always had – in their lifetime].

These financial "losers" also failed to calculate the effect on their payments when their sub-prime "teaser" mortgage rate moved to market rates or even well above market rates, or to calculate what would happen if housing prices dropped, or they lost their job – these "evil" people were "responsible" – **according to the spin** – for a sub-prime mortgage crisis of nearly $300 Billion. That's a lot of moola.

Now, in the game of Spin for you, the voter – "you the people" – discussion is supposed to stop here. Most of the rest of this is totally beyond your understanding, so let's not talk about it! That would upset the political process, and lead to a lot of **fact checking.** "Politics as usual" should not be about fact checking. That would just upset the narrative.

Still – something seems a bit strange here. Wasn't that sub-prime problem about $300 Billion? So if the government just bought those $300 Billion in bad mortgages – problem solved. But instead the Government has coughed up a lot more than that. By May of 2008, the number was $980 billion, and growing. What's going on? It was only $300 Billion for Pete's sake – well at least it was before the Slice and Dice game kicked in.

But by the time the geniuses of the financial world finished the slicing and dicing – first though CDOs and then through even more esoteric "spread the risk" financial wizardry called Credit Default Swaps (CDS), enabled and unregulated as an outcome of the CFMA, this $300 Billion had ballooned, according to Leopold, to an estimated $70 Trillion dollars! That is some 230 times as much as all of the real mortgage debt. Along the way, massive commissions and bonuses were generated, and duly banked in the Caymans or other suitable tax havens.

But as Leopold points out, because none of this trade was regulated, no one really knows for sure how big the problem is. Leopold refers to it as the "largest casino game in human history". Some observers have suggested the overall problem is much larger – up to $600 Trillion dollars.

Of course this whole $70+ Trillion mess is clearly the fault of those "street people" who thought it would be affordable and cozy to have a roof over their head!

And the Government, in a legitimate attempt to try to stave off a complete collapse like the Dirty Thirties, has been pumping your tax dollars into the same banking system that created the problem in the first place.

The judgment with respect to the practicality of that will have to wait for history, unless, of course it all gets flushed into the memory hole. Government is simply following the advice of the Fed (which you might recall is a cartel of bankers.)

Curiously enough, Leopold has not described this whole fiasco as a Ponzi scheme. That would make it not "financial wizardry" within the laws of the land, but a highly illegal criminal offence. And the bank officials who took money from the government as part of a Trillion dollar bailout, then proceeded in 2008 to pay themselves a bonus of some 18.4 Billion – well, most of them would be in jail!

In the sub-prime crisis, brokers and brokerage companies – many of whom should have known and many of whom undoubtedly did know that the derivatives were junk grade – were making unfair, deceptive, and un-true or misleading statements to clients. There should be restitution, with costs, for all such actions – not out of government coffers, but directly out of the broker's bank account – offshore or onshore – or through seizure and sale of assets. And just maybe, in some cases, really stiff jail terms.

Given the scale of the scheme, there is so much guilt to go around that it might require giving amnesty to the estimated 41,000 inmates of U.S. prisons currently serving time for marijuana offenses – in order to make room for the dozens of derivatives manufacturers and thousands of mortgage pushers and "toxic paper" pushers who are directly responsible for this worldwide disaster.

It would be a better way to use the space. The products these "tapeworms" pushed will ultimately be more disastrous than any batch of "ecstasy" mixed up in a toilet bowl, or cocaine pushed in Miami.

Yellow Sticky Note: Root problem – Investment bankers who have an "entitlement" gene and play "fantasy finance".

Blue Sticky Note: Proposed solution – Put them in jail, and get full restitution with costs. And again, don't treat them like some kind of celebrity.

My Notes for the Team Meeting: That the government should have bailed out these turkeys, with no real strings attached (e.g. thou shall actually start making business loans again, and immediately …) and with no prison time seems ludicrous to me. There certainly should be several dozen people – mainly senior execs from investment banks, not to mention the "raters" who provided high ratings on junk derivatives – who are candidates for striped pajamas.

Yellow Sticky Note: Root problem – Conflict of interest and depositor risk.

Blue Sticky Note: Proposed solution – Restore the forced separation between lending banks and investment banks that was originally in Glass-Steagall, and make it absolute.

My Notes for the Team Meeting: This is just restoring the position we were in from 1938 until Greenspan and the Fed decided to start loosening the rules in 1987, and then completely exposed your and my bank deposits to huge amounts of risk though the FSMA and CFMA in 1999-2000. This is as clear as daylight. Without the changes from 1987 to 2000, the sub-prime meltdown simply could not have occurred. Period!

So if this means breaking up some big banking organizations, and forcing divestiture of insurance and brokerage businesses, as was the case prior to 1987, so be it. Just watch really carefully during that process, because there are still more than a sufficient number of rotten apples in the barrel to engage in massive shell games during any reorganization. Oh yes, and take the reorganization costs out of the management salaries.

Green Sticky Note: What mechanisms could we set up to define and oversee this return to sanity?

And time for another **Cheerleader Award**, this one shared between Mr. Don Watkins and Dr. Yaron Brook, not surprisingly from the "Ayn Rand" center, and of course published in Forbes.com, 11/12/2012, on what they call the "Glass-Stegall Myth".

Interesting that they try to "halo brand" their piece of nonsense by showing a prominent photo of Nobel Prize winning economist Joseph Stiglitz, thereby implying that he agrees with their drivel, because they say he admitted that repeal of Glass-Stegall did not "directly cause" the crisis.

Of course they are right. Regulatory bills, or repeal of regulatory bills never directly cause crises. It's the greedy bastards that cause crises, aided and abetted by their Cheerleaders. I agree that we don't need regulations – once all of the greedy bastards are gone from the face of the earth. It is significant that Watkins and Brook make no positive suggestions backed by data, but allude in a grandiose way to other research. They also conveniently ignore or perhaps are not informed on the subject of the CFMA.

I didn't bother giving Forbes.com another Cheerleader award. I have read enough of the work posted to their pages to have come to the conclusion that they are the Faux News of the business world. They could pretty well rate a Cheerleader award any day of the week.

The Price-Fixing Gambit

And it goes on, and on. The Steal Game is just too profitable, and the ethical and moral standards of large numbers of owners and managers just way too low.

Because we have been conditioned to view rich white-collar folks as "successful" rather than as "tapeworms", when we do catch them we have a tendency to put them for a short time in reasonably fancy digs – rather than for a long time in the bowels of some filthy hole of a prison, which is where tapeworms really belong.

Barings management was roundly criticized during the Leeson affair for basically turning a blind eye while he made money for them (they thought) through very risky trades.

But the LIBOR scandal that unraveled in 2012 is a whole order of magnitude larger problem, involving collusion between bankers, and possibly some regulators, to play fast and loose with the London InterBank Offered Rate (LIBOR), a set of interest rates that is supposed to be calculated by rigorous methods – averaging data from a large number of sources.

According to Wikipedia, some $350 Trillion in derivatives and financial products are tied to the LIBOR rates. Check YouTube for "Libor and why should we care?" Turns out, you should care a lot, as the LIBOR rate affects mortgage rates, student loan rates, and small-business borrowing rates around the world.

No one has gone into the bowels of a prison, yet. Barclay's bank paid a £290 Million fine. This will surely make them more careful, when, for example, they booked a mere £11.6 Billion in profits in 2009, and paid a whopping 0.9 % (£113 Million) in taxes.

(So if Mitt Romney paid say between 13% and 15% taxes, he is really being ripped off, compared to the 0.9% that Barclays paid. What did you say your tax rate was?)

Barclays also saw their share price drop sharply, along with the share prices of Lloyds, HSBC, and Royal Bank of Scotland, who are all under investigation for collusion in the affair. Wonder if anybody knew in advance, and actually shorted the stock. Hmmm....

And they stand to lose more, with dozens of class action lawsuits in the U.S. alone alleging losses by plaintiffs resulting from the LIBOR manipulations. This will trickle down a lot of money – to lawyers.

I read an article a few days ago saying that the U.S. taxpayers would be on the hook for $3 Billion in losses at Fannie and Freddie because of the Libor manipulations. That $3 Billion, with penalties and interest should come directly out of the banks involved in the Libor manipulations, including seizure of assets, including personal assets of all those responsible. They won't need them when they are in jail anyway.

Next up, the Secured Creditors Game.

Notes: (Yellow: root cause; Blue: proposed solution; Green: question or additional data we need)

The rich are always going to say that, you know, just give us more money and we'll go out and spend more and then it will all trickle down to the rest of you. But that has not worked the last 10 years, and I hope the American public is catching on.
(Warren Buffett, from "www.brainyquote.com")

Chapter 13 – The Secured-Creditors Game

Also called the "some are more equal than others game", the secured creditors game is primarily played by bankers, private debt holders, and fund managers. This is not necessarily a bad thing, since these organizations are often playing the game with your money anyway – money from your savings account or pension plan. If they screw up badly, as they did in the mortgage crisis, everybody loses.

But that is not the usual situation. Where the secured-creditors game most frequently comes into play is in the end game, when the shell game is exposed and the kimono is opened. Now the secured-creditors – the ones we common shareholders **thought** were minding the store – walk in and extract their value from the company corpse with little or no loss. And the common shareholders get the leftovers – assuming there are any leftovers.

The Leftovers Game

To even get any of the leftovers, common shareholders have to engage in class actions. For this they need to engage class-action lawyers. Of course, like secured creditors, the lawyers eat a good chunk of the leftovers first, so the common shareholder ends up with the leftovers from the leftovers. Not very appetizing.

So when a company like Nortel goes down, what happens? Well first, the bulk of shareholders unload their stock, generally with huge losses (unless they are insider trading).

We know where most of that money ends up. When the truth starts to come out about the shell games, many of the unsecured shareholders join class action suits, hoping to get a few pennies on the dollar at the end of the process.

There are also large numbers of former employees who are holding stock options that were supposed to be part of their compensation for working tirelessly to make the company successful. These are now "underwater", meaning slightly less than worthless.

So then the company goes into "bankruptcy protection", which means that all of the companies to whom Nortel owed money, all of its suppliers and contractors, get into a queue for the leftovers.

These people are in a slightly better position than the shareholders, but still will be lucky to get 10 cents on the dollar. I've been there, in my own company, when my $4000 receivable (for training products to an electronics manufacturer who went into Chapter 11) turned into a few hundred when the dust settled.

The More Equal Than Others Mediation

Above virtually everyone in the queue are the Secured Creditors. They advanced often very large sums to companies such as Nortel, in exchange for an agreement to have first dibs on any money if things went wrong. Once the Chapter 11 is triggered, these secured creditors become part of the break-up and asset disposition – assets that were approximately $11.6 Billion against debt liabilities of $11.8 Billion, according to Nortel filings.

In the formal language of Bloomberg Business Week:

> "Nortel filed a Chapter 11 plan in July proposing full payment for secured creditors and distributions to lower-ranking creditors in accordance with priorities in bankruptcy law. There would be no distributions to creditors with subordinated claims."

("Lehman, Nortel, WaMu, General Growth: Bankruptcy", Bill Rochelle, Bloomberg Business Week, August 25, 2011)

Among the assets were some 6000 patents, which were to be auctioned off to the highest bidder.

So here we have some $11.6 Billion in assets at time of filing, but when the non-patent assets were sold off, they generated only about $3 Billion. The opening bid by Google on the patent assets was around a Billion. Oh-oh.

But, according to Benjamin Mak, a patent attorney with Ridout & Maybee LLP, speaking October 24, 2012 at the Medical Manufacturing Innovations Conference in Toronto, when the dust settled, the patent portfolio was purchased by a consortium of companies consisting of Apple/Microsoft/RIM for approximately $4.5 Billion. That makes a total of only $7.5 Billion to the good, against $11.8 Billion in liabilities. The math is pretty simple. Somebody loses big time.

Now the secured creditors are sitting around the mediation table, and they are looking at getting full payment. I have not in my web research been able to determine what the real number was in this case, but suppose that the secured creditors portion of the total debt was a hypothetical $2.95 Billion – that is 25% of the supposed asset value. From what I can see, this is not an unreasonable assumption at all, and could be driven much higher in companies that go on acquisition binges. (In the case of Four Seasons Healthcare, which we will discuss later, secured bondholders had 40%.)

Using a 25% estimate, we can see that the secured creditors can get their full $2.95 Billion back with no loss. With just one legal team reportedly getting $250,000 a month plus disbursements during the unwinding process, for most of the rest of the creditors, that leaves pretty much squat.

The Tax Break Gambit

One group of big losers in this was the Nortel pensioners. But government can take care of them, right? Now that would be the same government that provided Nortel with tax breaks, through the Scientific Research Tax Credit program, for a big chunk of the development cost of the intellectual property (IP) which is now the subject of the patent sale.

So the taxpayers of Canada in effect paid Nortel to develop the IP, and now that IP is sold off to mainly non-Canadian entities, to pay off largely non-Canadian secured creditors.

That's how it works. It's all legal. The secured creditors just want their money back as soon as possible – and they are the ones at the mediation table. It is pretty clear why companies like Nortel end up as part of a giant fire sale.

So the bottom line is that the Shell Game of getting really big by leveraging secured funds is not in employees', or shareholders', or suppliers', or the public's or the Governments' best interests.

But from the banker's perspective, would you rather manage one loan of $2 Billion to a huge multinational, or manage two thousand loans of $1 Million each to a bunch of small businesses run by owner managers who actually have a vested interest in the company's success? As long as you are "secured", the answer to that is a no brainer.

Cracking the Secured Creditor Eggs

Yellow Sticky Note: Root problem – some are more equal than others.

Blue Sticky Note: Proposed solution – require skin in the game and/or higher levels of due diligence and reporting.

My Notes for the Team Meeting: There are some trade-offs here, and the rules of the game are very different for different players. Bankers think funny – or don't think funny, depending on your perspective. If I went to my banker, and asked for a million dollar loan, he would want detailed business plans (which he might actually look at) specified collateral, and personal guarantees up the ying-yang. That's just what I would have to expect.

But if you are a big multinational, do the rules change? Personal guarantees? Not from a multinational, even if people who didn't understand "One of these is not like the other" actually think that a corporation is the same as a person. I guess bankers actually understood the show, although I am sure they identified more with the Count than a funny looking bird – even if they do sit on your nest egg. Five million beautiful dollars – ah, ha, ha, ha, ha!

Yellow Sticky Note: Root problem – due diligence by secured creditors.

Blue Sticky Note: Proposed solution – tie securitization level to due diligence and reporting.

My Notes for the Team Meeting: Due diligence? I am willing to bet there was less due diligence surrounding the loans to Nortel than there was to your mortgage loan. If there is a banker out there who can show proof positive that this is not the case, I welcome input for my next edition.

Now I did ask my banker about this. He is a good man, whom we have worked with for many years, and he assures me that the process is very similar to giving a loan to a small company.

But the problem that the bankers have is two fold. One is that they look at ratios, and at audited financial statements that they assume are correct. My Canadian bank lost something like 2.5 billion dollars in the Enron collapse, because they assumed that Arthur Anderson consulting was doing the job they were paid to do.

Is part of the problem that they assume too much, and don't apply **quite** the same criteria? Why would that be? Because the banks are secured. If things go terribly wrong, they go to the head of the queue. They cherry pick the assets, while everyone else including employees, shareholders, and pensionsers sit on the outside of the glass looking in.

So why go through too much trouble and expense of due diligence. A few quick ratios, a wink-wink nod-nod, and the deal is done, at least if the assets of the organization look much larger (on paper) than the money advance.

My banker did point out that secured creditors are behind the government in things like payroll and profit taxes, so they are not quite at the very top of the queue – just next in line. Of course by the time a company is going down, taxes on "profits" are pretty much a non-issue, and payroll taxes are monthly, so they cannot be too far out of line there either.

Now the bankers are the very folks that should be in a position to reassure us that the company is on the up and up, and a safe investment for the rest of us. It would be nice if I could ring up the bank and say, "Look, you just handed these guys $2.5 Billion to leverage their buy out of XYZ company. You've had a look under the kimono. Is this a safe investment?". "Sorry, client privilege".

So I think the rule should be, that when things implode, the first question the receiver asks is: "Show me the documentary evidence that you really did your due diligence. Oh. So you don't have that proof handy? How inconvenient. Get in line with everyone else."

Green Sticky Note: What would this look like? What should be required to show proof of real due diligence? What disclosures should be required? That should keep the Senate Banking Committee going for a while.

My Notes for the Team Meeting: When Nortel filed for protection, they did so because they had an interest payment of something like $107 Million coming due. Yes, I said *interest* payment. Knowing that the interest rates at the time were very low by historical standards up until then, you can play with the math.

But if the bank creditors did not have iron clad assurance that the receiver would rule in their favor on the subordination thing, might Nortel have had some negotiation room and additional time to turn things around?

But then, given the Nortel management strategy of the time, they might have just dug the hole deeper, which is probably why the banks did not give them more time.

Yellow Sticky Note: Root problem – Intellectual Property leaves the country of origin, even though taxpayers have heavily supported it.

Blue Sticky Note: Proposed solution – Treat all taxpayer input (subsidies, tax credits) as a loan.

Monologue: *"You want government money? Scientific research tax credits? Subsidies? No problem. You do understand the rules? Yes. All of this money goes on your books as secured long-term debt".*

*"No, it is not callable under any circumstances, **unless** you screw up, and crash and burn – at which point 'we the people' are at the front of the line, and have first call on any IP you have developed with public money."*

"All other debt, including big bank debt, is subordinated to this. Oh? Your private bankers won't like this? Tell you what. Get the money you need from them. I'm sure we can find other companies that could use what we have to offer."

That finishes my set of sticky notes drawn from observation of the Secured Creditors Game. Have you added yours? Next up, the big G of Government.

Notes: (Yellow: root cause; Blue: proposed solution; Green: question or additional data we need)

"I am only one, but I am one. I cannot do everything, but I can do something. And because I cannot do everything, I will not refuse to do the something that I can do. What I can do, I should do. And what I should do, by the grace of God, I will do."
(Edward Everett Hale {April 3, 1822 – June 10, 1909} American author, historian and Unitarian clergyman.)

"Chains of habit are too light to be felt until they are too heavy to be broken."
(Warren Buffett, from "www.brainyquote.com")

Chapter 14 – A New Face for Government

The cures that can salvage capitalism and save democracy in the process are conceptually very simple, but for a government to put them in place, and/or for Capitalists with the moral persuasion of Adam Smith to put them in place will take a concerted effort. To get these groups to move at all will take intensive pressure from those who see where the current slippery slope is heading – and who stand up and shout "Enough Already!" And this needs to happen now, not five years from now.

The alternative is to wait passively for the arrival of a new Dark Age of Orwellian dimensions – to drop into your armchair, tune in the latest game show, grab your GMO corn chips and a beer, and say "I'm alright Jack".

We have already moved so far down the road towards global corporatism that only very strong government action can even hope to stop the mad dash to doom. So to fix capitalism, we first have to fix government.

We have all been lulled into an easy complacence by a steady diet of "bread and circuses". It really doesn't matter if you think this is part of a grand plot to grab control of totalitarian power, suitable for the next Dan Brown thriller, or just the natural result of an improved standard of living and life of comparative ease that we have had in North America since the end of World War II. The result has been the same.

Spectator Sport

If we are to head off disaster for 99.5% of the human population, we need to get engaged. We are the ones that we have been waiting for. We need to stop being spectators and get in the game – particularly that wonderful game called politics. It is interesting that many of the new democracies around the world have very high voter participation, whereas in America it has been declining for years.

I have seen an article – by a person who left a well-placed political-insider position – that claims the drop in voter participation is by design, that the political party of which he was a part has been deliberately manipulating the electorate to actually lower voter participation. Not good, when you realize how low voter participation is already.

A Wikipedia list of voter participation compiled for the period from 1960 to 1995 (based on Statistics concerning electoral participation from Mark N. Franklin's <u>Controversies in Voting Behavior</u>, 2001) shows a disturbing set of numbers. Voter participation for the countries listed shows Canada is in 30th spot and the U.S in 39th. Against peers in the G8, Canada comes in fifth – ahead of Japan, Russia, and the U.S. The U.S. was dead last, by a long shot – Russia 61% and U.S. 48%.

In new democracies in the Middle East and Asia, where people don't take good government for granted, citizens go to the polls in defiance of violence and death threats. Meanwhile, here on our side of the lake, many North American "couch coaches" can't pull themselves out of the armchair and away from the game shows or football long enough to vote, let alone take the very substantial effort to research the issues in advance.

But it's fine and appropriate to complain with the boys over a beer about how the politicians have screwed us over. "Well I didn't vote for that rat!" *(Translation: "I was home watching the rerun of the Cowboy's game, and just couldn't find time to vote.")*

To really take back control of the situation, however, means going beyond the relatively simple process of voting – which should not even be a question – and engaging in the processes that select candidates for a party. If this is left to a minority of people with unpleasant agendas, then you will end up with candidates with unpleasant agendas.

The Tea Party extremism of the current election is a case in point. Candidates have been largely screened by their position on various religious, discriminatory, and frankly racist issues – even as the economy has been in free fall, and democratic freedoms we have taken for granted – freedoms enshrined in our constitutions – are under fierce assault.

These two issues of candidate selection and actual voting are clearly related. If you really believe you are choosing between a scumbag and a crook, you are more likely to sit it out with your corn chips – not that you should – because even here there are degrees of scummy-ness and different levels of honor among thieves. Not voting, or voting for "none of the above" might make one feel superior and above all that dirt, but is generally useless in terms of improving things.

The Party

At the opposite end of the spectrum from the "couch coach" non-voter, is the "reflex voter". Now a reflex, in simple terms, is an action that happens from stimulus to response without ever passing through the brain – like what happens when the doctor taps below your kneecap to see if your leg jerks. Doesn't take much brain.

Reflex voters vote for whomever the Party puts forward.

"Vote? Yessiree. My grandpappy's pappy, and my grand pappy, and my pappy always voted (Democrat/ Republican/ Liberal/ Conservative – fill in the blank), and that's how I vote too! {Smile broadly} It's in our genes."

Well something is in the genes ok. So much so, that reflex voters don't even notice when the whole party gets hijacked, sometimes even changing the party name in the process. That happened in Canada. People whose pappy's pappy voted for the Progressive Conservative Party (PCs) in the 1960's still vote today for the presumed "successor" Conservative Party of Canada.

These reflex voters have not noticed that this Conservative party played a game of leap-frog to the right, finally clearing right over the top of the (now defunct) Reform Party of Canada (for whom these reflexive types would never have voted in a million years), and landing squarely in the next-most position to Fascism in the conventional seven-step left-to-right political spectrum that many of us learned in school:

Communist –> Social Democrat –> Progressive –> Liberal
–> Conservative –> Reactionary –> Fascist

In fact, if you want to know where the old PC Party fell in the spectrum, mix one part Progressive and one part Conservative and you end up with (drum roll) Liberal – which is pretty much why voters often said there was not much difference between the two parties' policies over time. Am I happy that our present Prime Minister's party is now barely to the left of Fascist? No, not really.

In the U.S., this whole spectrum thing seems to break down, because the terms get thrown around with gay abandon.

Some of this looks a lot like Orwellian newspeak, such as communistfascist. I have spent way too many hours on Internet "comments" trying to explain that these are not the same – that there are very fundamental differences in the philosophies of Hitler and Stalin, and in the structure of both the government and the society each created.

Both Hitler and Stalin were megalomaniacs, both were morally bankrupt, and both ran totalitarian states, but those are about the only things they had in common, which has mainly to do with their psychology and ethics, not their politics. Their political spectrum differences (plus some "resource" considerations) were the main reason they tore at each other like mad dogs during WWII.

The spectrum thing also breaks down in a two party system (which the U.S., de-facto, is) because people seem to lose the ability to understand the nuances. So everyone who is right of liberal is conservativefascist, and everyone liberal or anywhere left of that is communistliberal.

One of the interesting consequences of this reasoning is that in spite of the triumph over communism, this makes virtually all of the developed nations outside of North America, the ones with better healthcare and lower child mortality rates – well quite frankly, communistliberal!

Using newspeak tends to hinder dialog just a smidgen. It does make it a lot easier for some members of the press corp, because they don't need to be nearly as analytical, and it reduces the need to try to understand or try to describe any nuances at all. And it makes it much easier for the scumbags to control us.

Whipping Up a New-Politics Recipe

I almost called this Whipping Up a New Deal, but "New Deal" was already taken, so let's just go with "recipe". Some of the ingredients "we the people" can supply, and we need to do that first. Otherwise, nothing will change.

The recipe is also slightly different North and South of our respective borders, but not that different in practice. **And this will not be a quick fix** – say for example one-half of the next Presidential term. In politics there seldom is, nor should there necessarily be, instant gratification. But during a full Presidential term, and absent Congressional gridlock, we might start to role back some of the worst of the abuses.

First, if you have not already done so, figure out how to vote for the candidate, not the party. And start with honesty, integrity, and caring. If your Congressman or MP is a dishonest S.O.B, don't vote for him. If he was caught cheating on his expense account, or if he is arrogant and lacking in understanding, or he tried to dodge taxes, or he ducked out on military service when your country was at risk, don't vote for him. Come to think of it, it is a bit like picking a new CEO.

If he will do these things, then he has decided that he is "entitled", and you don't really count for much, even if you did contribute to his campaign. I'm sure you have all heard the story of the sweet young thing who was asked: *"If I gave you a million dollars, would you sleep with me?"* to which she answered, "A Million dollars! Why sure!" … *"So how about a hundred bucks?"* … "What do you think I am, a prostitute?!!" *"We have already established that. Now we are just haggling over the price."*

Political prostitutes sleep with the highest bidder, and sometimes the barrier to entry is pretty thin.

If a candidate is a political prostitute, don't vote for him. Not unless you have unlimited funds, and enjoy being a part of the problem. Let him go to work for a living. If you would not hire him to work in a responsible and low-oversight job in your company, why would you even dream of letting him near a vote on important government legislation that could affect you, your children, and your children's children?

And if a political prostitute gets into office anyway, watch him or her like a hawk. Press your local journalists hard to keep tabs. Follow up any awkward spots with enquiry – where there is smoke, there is usually fire. Use freedom of information legislation, friends of friends who are on the inside – whatever it takes. Attend meetings. Ask awkward questions.

Don't cross any lines that might open you up to legal action, but exercise freedom of speech – while you still have it! Join with circles of like-minded people to increase the heat. Where necessary, create and/or support petitions through socially responsible organizations like Avaaz to shed light on the issues and encourage rectification of wrongdoing.

There are thousands of voters in every riding or congressional district. If one-half-of-one-percent of the electorate took some time away from the "bread and circuses" to keep tabs on these political twits, the crooks would not last long. And the ones who are considering crossing the line? They will sit up straight and take notice. *"Don't know if you noticed, but Rip Van Voter has woken from his slumber, and is actually watching!"*

Yellow Sticky Note: Root problem – Politicians who befriend crooks.

Blue Sticky Note: Proposed solution – Judge and vote for individual politicians by the friends they keep.

My Notes for the Team Meeting: Kenneth Lay was, as Arianna Huffington puts it, a "FOG (friend of George)". In her Internet paper "Enron: Cooking The Books And Buying Protection" she summarizes the problem as follows:

> "The Enron debacle has exposed the dark side of capitalism -- and the unseemly link between money and political influence. Let's hope it also sheds a light on the desperate need for fundamental campaign finance reform. Because trust in the fundamental decency of our political system is not a trivial, inside-the-Beltway issue. Just ask the scores of people who were being sold on the virtues of investing their golden years in Enron -- right up until the stock crashed."

Yellow Sticky Note: Root problem – politicians who are bought and paid for.

Blue Sticky Note: Proposed solution – Judge and vote for the party and/or the individual politicians who will vote in favor of campaign finance reform.

Cracking Some Constitutional Eggs

In 1867 in Canada, and 1776 in the U.S., our respective founding fathers, faced with the realities of the times, devised a government structure that seemed like it should serve us well, and it has done so remarkably for a substantial period of time. Interestingly, we in Canada patterned ours after Mother England, and you in the U.S. patterned yours Auntie England.

So we have a Constitutional Monarchy, with a Prime Minister, Parliament, and Senate and you have a Republic, with a separate Executive branch, and a Legislative Branch consisting of Senate and House of Representatives.

Now we "walk on eggs" if we think about … even discussing … the slightest possibility … of changing any of the way this works. It's in the constitution for Pete's sake!

That might be, and there was a time in history, when conditions were substantially different, when the system probably made sense. Part time "congressmen" actually worked for a living most of the year, meeting only occasionally to transact National business.

> *The Congress shall assemble at least once in every Year, and such Meeting shall be on the first Monday in December, unless they shall by law appoint a different Day.*

> [Article I, Section 4, clause 2 of 1787 Constitutional Convention in Philadelphia]

When ballot boxes arrive for counting on horseback or by stagecoach, certain allowances have to be made. Perhaps the conditions have changed a tad since 1787. And some really big advances have been made.

The Representation Play

One of our big values, in Western democracies is, well, democracy! Since the days when a bunch of nobles on big horses, with some armed friends around them, forced King John of England to sign the Magna Carta, or Great Charter of Freedoms, things improved over the years. But freedom for some – not all – was problematic in many ways. If we believe that the role of government is to see to the well being of the entire populace, then the entire populace has to be represented.

In the 1750's, the peoples of the American colonies were not well represented in London, and as a result, taxation issues (the movement of goods and services) and the flow of money were kinda out of whack. One of the defining slogans of the time was "no taxation without representation". In 1773, the tea went into Boston harbor, and the rest "is history", as they say.

In 1776, if you were born female, or black, take voting day off. Your services were not required. So in the 20th century we made some big gains, but problems remain.

Fast forward to 2012. Look back at the games that have been played since the end of WWII, and the taxation, movement of goods and services, and the flow of money. Are you truly "represented" in government? Are your "representatives" primarily there to bring value for you, the true owner and customer of government?

I don't think so either. The government "of the people for the people" has become the government "of the rich for the rich", and we have let that happen on our watch. The tea has been poured; time to break some more eggs.

The "First Past the Post" Egg

There have been many laments from U.S. voters in the last few months about having to vote either Republican or Democratic. Shouldn't there be a reasonable third option? To this, my Canadian response is – be careful what you wish for! Bin dere, done dat, got the tee shirt.

Canada currently has five different parties represented in the House of Commons, and a government that does not even come close to representing the will of the people. How is that possible? Because of a perversion of democracy (which might have made some sense, at some time, maybe???) called "first past the post" – and the resulting "spoiler effect".

When you add in the fun and games of riding boundaries in Canada, and the electoral college system in the U.S., mix in hanging chad in Florida, or voter fraud in dozens of ridings in Canada – which clearly broke Canadian laws during our last Federal Election – and we have the recipe for deep doo-doo. Slugs and tapeworms thrive in doo-doo.

With our present Canadian system and three major parties, one regional (ethnic) party, and one environmentalist party, we are almost never going to get a politician who is the choice of even close to 50% of the population.

So in 2006, the Harper government got in with 36% of the votes cast, and 124 seats against 3 opposition parties, who between them had 184 seats. This "minority government" has much the same effect in Canada as dividing the House of Representatives and Senate control in the U.S. Not quite the same – but sort of.

Not liking to operate with a minority, where he had to actually listen to other peoples' opinions, Harper cashed in his chips and had the Governor General agree to call another election in 2008. Courtesy of more split votes, Harper snagged another 1.38% of the vote – but that netted him a 15% gain in seats.

Now in this 2008 election, there were some clearly illegal election-spending issues, for which the Conservative Party was ultimately "fined" a small sum. About as much deterrent as the Barclay fine for the LIBOR malfeasance.

Apparently the reflex voters were not paying attention. Crooks are crooks, and prostitutes are prostitutes. In the 2011 election, which was marked by "irregularities" (the Robocall scandal) leading to voter complaints in over 200 ridings and 1500 polling stations, Harper pulled in another 1.95% of the vote, and gained an additional 16% of the seats.

So from 2006 up to 2011, and ignoring the impacts of voter fraud, **a tiny 3.33% change in popular vote resulted in a massive 33.9% change in number of seats**, giving Harper a majority - which in 2012 Canada, more or less makes him the Sun King or the Great Leader, with a whip! This is the magic of "First Past the Post" (FPTP).

Does "First Past the Post" affect the U.S.? At the Presidential level, it certainly does! From the election of Thomas Jefferson in 1800 up to the 1912 election of Woodrow Wilson, and from the 1980 election of Ronald Reagan up to the election of George W. Bush in 2000, spoiler candidates "decided" eleven presidential elections.

Without consumer rights crusader Ralph Nader, Al Gore would have been standing on that aircraft carrier proclaiming "Mission Accomplished", or maybe not. Maybe there would not have been an Iraq War at all.

But what the heck! The Iraq war cost only a few thousand American lives, a few hundred thousand Iraqi ones, and $807 billion in taxes on "we the people", before interest charges. Not a big deal. So thanks for the good intentions, Ralph. In hindsight, would you have intentionally swung the vote in this direction? Did you anticipate the outcome, or did you put on a set of blinders in order to be "right"?

I need to be clear here that the problem is not that someone disagrees with the two default parties but that the FPTP system in effect punishes the dissident opinions. Folks such as Nader in the U.S., the Greens, and even the Bloc Quebecois in Canada, are attempting to change things, to represent people concerned with perceived shortcomings in the existing parties.

But the ultimate end result is that their efforts result in less representation for the people, thanks to the brilliant gambit of First Past the Post. (And just in passing, if you check the records, there were no "spoilers" in U.S. Presidential Elections between 1912 and 1980).

Yellow Sticky Note: Root problem – taxation (and imposition of other unfair rules and practices) without representation.

Blue Sticky Note: Proposed solution – eliminate FPTP and replace with proportional representation and/or preferential balloting and/or elimination balloting (multiple rounds dropping the candidate with the least votes at each round).

Yellow Sticky Note: Root problem – crooks and political prostitutes in power.

Blue Sticky Note: Proposed solution – don't stop at fining them. Throw the party out of power, and the specific perpetrators in jail, and do it now, not three years of legal bull and another election later.

Blue Sticky Note: Proposed solution – politicians caught clearly accepting bribes and accepting favors in return for their votes should be banned from any level of public office – for life.

Now we need many more sticky notes here. We need a lot of team input! Get the thinking caps cranked to maximum power, because getting there from here is not going to be an easy sell, or an easy trip.

The "Support the Party" Egg

According to www.house.gov, the role of a U.S. Congressman is as follows:

> "Elected to a two-year term, each representative serves the people of a specific congressional district by introducing bills and serving on committees, among other duties."

Hmmm. So explain to me how, at the beginning of a congressional session, stating as your goal an attempt to limit the current President to one term is "serving the people"? Here I thought all along that "the people" would make the choice of whether or not a President should serve a second term, and that fiscal arm-twisting to affect their decision on such things is not kosher.

And explain to me again how filibustering budget bills until S&P downgrades the credit rating of the U.S. Government, coincidentally making Government borrowing more expensive, and thus adding to the peoples' tax bill, "serves the people". It might be almost defensible if it really was about "entitlement" of the 47%, and not a consequence of the massive Steal Game that was going on starting before 2000.

I used to be really impressed watching bipartisan debates on C-Span where Democrats and Republicans stood up and spoke in support of a bill, and other Democrats and Republicans stood up and spoke against the same bill, and both parties worked toward making it a better piece of legislation. And then at the end of it, congressmen voted their conscience, and the bill stood or fell on its' merits.

One almost never sees that kind of bipartisan behavior broadcast here in Canada. Instead we have an "unreality game show" called question period, in which the goal is to score political points for your side by either "embarrassing" the government if you are in opposition, or showing how creative you can be in finding ways to not answer the question, if you are on the government side of the house. (Sort of a reverse version of the 2012 Presidential debates). And we pay the actors in these charades some pretty significant coin for "entertaining" us in this manner.

Mind you, in the British parliamentary tradition, politicians can vote their conscience, rather like that bipartisan support of a given bill. This is actually called a "free vote" – which kind'a suggests that all the other votes are not free. Rather, they are bought and paid for by the Party or by Party supporters. Most recent votes in Canada are of this latter kind.

But some politicians actually do have a conscience, and might just vote in a way that does not toe the party line. So they need to be "whipped into shape" like unruly slaves. For this, the party uses the "Party Whip". Yup, that's what he (or she) is actually called! The Party Whip! The whole concept behind this is that the Party makes the rules, the Party is always right, and you will bloody well do what the Party wants, or else.

And the "or else" can get pretty brutal, from kicking you out of cabinet back to the back-benches (Canada), or kicking you off of committees where you might otherwise help draft or vet legislation (Canada and the U.S.), right though to much more extreme actions – such as arranging for slander and slur that ultimately gives the Party "cover" to boot you out of the Party altogether, or at least greatly dim your hopes of re-election.

This has happened under Harper several times, and although there have been lawsuits against the party by former members so aggrieved, it has allowed him to continue his march to the right, unfettered by any need to concern himself with "Red Tories" – another piece of communist-under-the-bed "newspeak" invented way back in the days of the centrist Joe Clark PC government.

And if the Party can't whip you into shape though these short term solutions, the "final solution" is political death by Primary firing squad. (Riding associations in Canada. With somewhat tighter gun laws, riding associations get on big horses and trample anyone who is a threat to the Party hierarchy and political position).

Control the primaries, or riding associations – control the candidates. Control the candidates, control the Party makeup. Control the Party makeup, control the House vote, control the agenda, and control the World. So if "we the people" want to really have representative government, there are some Party eggs to be broken.

Yellow Sticky Note: Root problem – whipping of representatives to support bad legislation that they don't believe in.

Blue Sticky Note: Proposed solution – improve transparency.

Blue Sticky Note: Proposed solution – provide solid legal protection for individual conscientious legislators from arbitrary punishment.

Blue Sticky Note: Proposed solution – provide substantial penalties for coercion.

Yellow Sticky Note: Root problem – Joe public not noticing, or turning his back when the "good guys" get whipped.

Blue Sticky Note: Proposed solution – pay attention.

Blue Sticky Note: Proposed solution – speak out publicly in support of the honest guy.

Blue Sticky Note: Proposed solution – don't reflex vote.

Blue Sticky Note: Proposed solution – support "conscientious objectors", especially in the preliminary events.

Yellow Sticky Note: Root problem – Parties!

Blue Sticky Note: Proposed solution – In today's technological age, maybe we don't even need Parties at all.

Green Sticky Note: How could we accomplish the current perceived-useful "party" role with a totally different mechanism?

Yellow Sticky Note: Root problem – The Media!

Blue Sticky Note: Proposed solution – Demand better coverage and analysis, including fact checking. Hire more educated columnists, and pay the political, economics, and business columnists a wage that is at least as much as the sports guy.

My Notes for the Team Meeting: Consider the various sources of news that you regularly visit. Compare the advertisers and the news articles. Do you sense a connection? If a 2-page coal ad and an article supporting mountain top removal co-exist, can you trust the independence of the source?

It is an unfortunate aspect of capitalism that the news magazines and programs depend on advertising for funding, and therefore tend to avoid dumping on the practices of the advertiser. Caveat Lector has never been more applicable.

Blue Sticky Note: Proposed solution – Protect the media sources that are independent of advertising. This is critical to having unbiased sources.

Blue Sticky Note: Don't allow huge media conglomerates to form. Adhere to strict rules related to the size of media empires and concentration of control in specific markets.

My Notes for the Team Meeting: In Canada, there is currently a big fight to save the CBC, a National radio/TV network funded with public money and largely devoid of advertising. Some rather amazing interviews bring in experts from all sides of controversial issues.

When CEOs or politicians refuse to be interviewed, this is also transparent. Is it surprising that our current slightly-right-of-Attila-the-Hun Conservative Government is trying to control them by cutting funding? The message is clear – "Cross me and you could be out of a job, and I will claim I am just protecting taxpayer money."

Expect a similar assault on organizations like PBS, and small independents that would like to tell you the truth, but are very vulnerable.

Yellow Sticky Note: Root problem – How we use the media!

Blue Sticky Note: Proposed solution – Shift our collective focus – away from the bread and circuses to what is happening when we are not watching. Move beyond 90-second sound bytes to engage in real dialogue and multiple viewpoints.

Green Sticky Note: How much of a problem is this? Can we get some measures? Could we track this over time? Would knowing the data actually wake us up about the process?

My Notes for the Team Meeting: Advertisers ensure a healthy dose of sports and fashion, trivializing the big issues. Through coupons, contests, and commentaries on the lives of the stars, they keep us engaged in entertainment, and reduce us to the level of judging the players, the game moves, the survivors, and the dance competitions. This was bad enough **before** the days of Internet games on Facebook.

Maybe we should try an experiment, sort of like a diet or exercise program! Take 15-30 minutes a day. Read the news – local, national, and international. Yes, this includes what is happening in other countries. Digest it. Ponder it. Ask, "why?" And follow significant stories from week to week. Will we find it increasingly easy for the sports or entertainment section to wait until after the main meal?

I admit I might be treading on some sacred ground here. But here is a challenge to analyze what is going down. Watch people in a crowd – in a hotel lobby or on an airplane or train, where newspapers are passed out free.

Tally the numbers who:
(1) look at any news other than the headlines – I mean actually read an article in depth;
(2) actually turn to page two to finish an article, having already skimmed the headlines and the "juicy" parts in the very first paragraph;
(3) just pick up the paper, flip to the (a) sports page or (b) arts and entertainment page (gossip), and discard the rest of the paper.

Green Sticky Note: Are we, as a society, fixated on "bread and circuses" , and how bad a fixation is this? Are we collectively paying attention to all the wrong things, while the crooks and worms grab the family silver and run for it?

My Notes for the Team Meeting: If you are either really brave, or just really obtuse like me, try to start a conversation on a bus or plane about any one of the topics that we have covered in this book. **Warning:** if person B is wearing an Armani suit, a genuine Rolex, and looks like he might have a hairpiece, try to make sure he is not "carrying" before you start the conversation, or that the guy in the next seat in not an "enforcer".

If you are comfortable, you could try some really common icebreaker, such as: "Did you know that when he was twenty-four years old, Alan Greenspan was a acolyte of Ayn Rand?" If they reply "Who is Alan Greenspan", then I suggest you switch to football.

Green Sticky Note: How do we get though to friends and acquaintances who live for Sunday football or can't switch off "The Price is Right", while their children's inheritance – and democracy itself – is being snatched from under their noses?

Big Billed Birds Egg

When you pick though the "Scrambled Eggs Super" of today's massive legislative bills, you find lots of stuff that should not be in "your food". Probably the worst example in recent human history, and maybe in all time everywhere, is the 450-page Canadian Bill C38 – the Conservative Budget Implementation Act 2012 – also called by critics the "Trojan Horse" bill.

Given control of the majority of seats in the commons, by legal or illegal means, the Harper government literally rammed through a supposed "budget bill" which includes, among other things changes that:

- gut 20-years worth of previous environmental protection gains;
- weaken the government science community in everything from climate and pollution monitoring and fisheries protection to demographics and statistics;
- seek to limit, through changes in the Income Tax Act, the ability of charitable organizations to engage in any kind of political activities;
- wipe out a backlog of 280,000 immigration applications by skilled immigrants;
- change the oversight of the Canadian Security Intelligence Service;
- shut down government funding to citizen-based health and welfare groups, rights and democracy groups, and environmental groups; and
- make significant changes to the social security and employment insurance programs.

And they rammed this Trojan Horse though by passing a motion to limit debate to something like ten hours on this massive bill. Incredible.

As one recent comment on a news feed succinctly put it:

> "Harper and the cons are in a huge rush to bypass democracy. It really does get in their way. It is such an inconvenience."

From my understanding, such an atrocious bill could not (presently) ever make it though both the U.S. Congress and Executive branch. The U.S. Constitution provides some checks and balances, and earlier Congressional leaders have put in place procedures that should make this abuse of power very difficult.

But you do have provisions in those same procedural rules that result in massive abuse, and that cost the taxpayer big time. That is the provision for "pork-barrel politics" through "earmarks" – funding designations tacked onto totally unrelated bills as the price of support by specified congressmen.

Outside of politics, this would be called "extortion", or at the very least vote buying – but inside the halls of Congress this is just business as usual.

And of course these earmarks are intended by that congressman to reward big campaign contributors, or to effectively "buy" votes from his constituency. And Sen. Phil Gramm did get the CFMA tacked onto a budget bill.

In the Harper case, Bill C-38 is in large part to support large resource projects like mining and tar-sands export, which will certainly benefit a few big corporations to the tune of billions of dollars, and has and will contribute big time to Conservative campaign funds. In any context except politics, this would all fall under the illegal activity called bribery.

Yellow Sticky Note: Root problem – crooks and political prostitutes in power.

Blue Sticky Note: Proposed solution – (See previous sections!)

Yellow Sticky Note: Root problem – supersized, toxic, and "Trojan Horse" bills.

Blue Sticky Note: Proposed solution – Limit bill size and "earmarks".

Blue Sticky Note: Proposed solution – remove the direct influence of corporations in wording of bills.

Blue Sticky Note: Proposed solution – restrict the content of and amendments to a proposed bill to things that actually pertain to the main purpose of that bill.

Blue Sticky Note: Proposed solution: Prevent the inclusion in a bill of clauses that would have the effect of nullifying other bills, without full debate on the intent and purpose of the original bill.

My Notes for the Team Meeting: All of these things must pass into law, and none will happen unless we make them happen. Recall Edward Everett Hale's wonderful quote at the start of this chapter:

> "I am only one, but I am one. I cannot do everything, but I can do something. And because I cannot do everything, I will not refuse to do the something that I can do. What I can do, I should do. And what I should do, by the grace of God, I will do."

So we must first be true to ourselves and do what we should do. But we are also a part of a great brotherhood of man, so we are one but we are also many, millions around the world.

If we can't move mountains by ourselves, we can leverage the many, within our social groups, on petition sites like Care2Action, and Avaaz, though networks of likeminded people on Facebook or Linked In, on chat groups and newsgroups, and in our community groups and grassroots political organizations.

The "Sue The Government Into Submission" Fallacy

One last thing, which is really an afterthought, is prompted by an email I recently received from a cause that I definitely believe in – Ecojustice. I was well into the last chapter of this tome, so backtracking "smarts", but this is an important point.

To make things happen, and pull us out of the quicksand that we are slowly but surely sinking into, one approach is to go the "legal action" route and sue the twits in Government when they break their own rules.

Now this seems a sensible and reasonable thing to do. Without statistical studies, and in my usual cavalier way, I will go with my gut – and some very direct local experience over the past two years and say, in most of these cases going "legal" against the government will backfire.

[Hopefully someone out there will grab this one as an "opportunity" and actually gather some real data, rather than my anecdotal stuff and bunches of hunches. Hint: This would make a good Masters or Ph.D. study for some enterprising person in the environmental or sustainability space.]

Why would this backfire, you might well ask? All we are doing is seeking to use the law directly against the government, so they do what the law requires, and do the right thing!

I have seen this one close up, in a local battle with the City of Ottawa, over the destruction of an ecologically sensitive area of pristine forest and wetlands on the west end of town. (I could give you about 600 reasons this should not have happened/be happening, but that is totally beside the point.)
The problems with the "go legal" approach are many, but when you think about it, the first one is the real biggy:

1. You are really suing yourself and your friends, and your "could be" friends and supporters. To me, this seems just a bit dumb. If you win big, what are the newspaper headlines?

- *"City Loses Courts Case Against the Environuts Coalition – Settlement Will Cost Taxpayers $400,000."*
- *"Two Years After Completion of Highway, Court Case Finally Settled"*
- *"Mayor Cites Legal Costs, Cost Overruns From Construction Delays, in Defending Tax Increases."*

Does this really help the cause? It does not seem a winning gambit if your long-term goal is to gain friends, influence people, and affect real change.

All of those people on the margins, the ones you might have recruited in your fight against City Hall – now they hate your guts. Yes, they don't understand what is at stake. Yes, they should, but they don't.

And the media, and the social media trolls, and government "attack poodles" as Catherine Austin Fitts calls them, will make sure the public continues to not understand the real issues.

2. You are making heroes out of bums. The City is not messing up the environment; it is "protecting the taxpayer".

3. The City (or Province/State or Federal Government) makes the laws. They have spent years dancing with moneyed folks in the private sector, either weakening the laws or making them so obtuse that any attempt at holding them accountable has about a snowball's chance in hell of getting anywhere – and will cost an arm and a leg.

4. If you do actually succeed in pinning them on this one, what do you think their response will be? Say,
   a. *"Oh we are so sorry, we won't be bad again."* Or
   b. *"We need to change that law, so we can't be caught that way again".*

Maybe that is why there is a current discussion on the Green forums in Linked In that asks:

> "Are environmental standards, and the laws and research resources that support them being systematically dismantled to push the fossil fuels agenda?"

5. The legal process, at least as currently constituted, has all sorts of procedural delay tactics built in. These are supposed to protect a defendant from being railroaded, but in fact primarily serve the purpose of making the case drag on and on, while the lawyer's bill is climbing rapidly.

This works against you, because the Government has a whole passel of lawyers who work for them and view their job as "protecting the government", not protecting the public – unlimited time and basically unlimited funds.

We could get caught up in the niceties of this, but the bottom line is that "we the people" are paying for both sides of the legal argument – one through voluntary donations, calendar sales, and bake sales, and one though the involuntary donations called taxes. What could possibly be a better example of lose-lose for "we the people".

6. Even if the court supports your position, as they did in aspects of our reference case:
   a. the damage is already done (road is built, and trees cleared on the highlands for more little boxes made of ticky-tacky);
   b. the court is not obligated to award you costs (they didn't); and
   c. you are stuck with a huge legal bill, on which the lawyer charges interest (yes he does).

No one who was not part of the original questionable decision to "go legal" in the first place is overly keen on paying the bills for a "lost cause" after the fact, and the more desperate your attempts to recoup these costs and get the lawyer off your back, the more you fragment and alienate parts of what should be your support base.

You have now dug a huge hole, jumped in with both feet, and rendered yourself considerably less effective in the future.

Yellow Sticky Note: Root problem – Suing the Government for wrong doing, such as ignoring their own laws, does not seem to work that well.

Blue Sticky Note: Proposed solution – If you must "go legal", go after the organization that stands to **benefit** from breaking the law, the corporations, not the government.

My Notes for the Team Meeting: Often companies have falsified information, or ignored inconvenient truths, "strong-armed" consultants into cooking the data, etc. Try to get the government (and government lawyers) on your side of the legal table, or at the least, make it very politically inconvenient for them to side with the crooks.

Concentrate your arguments in the media on the perpetrators, not on their government backers. You and I both know that in these situations, the taxpayer will ultimately lose.

Make it about taxes! Make it about hidden infrastructure costs. Make it about externalized costs. (OK – so that is what happens when you go back and insert stuff. The "externalized-cost time bomb" is in the next Chapter. ☹)

Blue Sticky Note: Proposed solution – Don't go legal. Go PR. Public demonstrations, legal information sessions, picketing, handouts.

And control the message, the same way that governments and businesses do. No loose cannons (I'm bad this way – so please do what I say, not what I do ☹).

Get ahead of the curve and be ready with press releases and all of the necessary support for the media before launch. Don't allow yourself to become strictly reactive and off-balance.

Notes: (Yellow: root cause; Blue: proposed solution; Green: question or additional data we need)

"Despite all its shortcomings, this Constitution looms ... as the only work of liberty which Eastern Europe has ever created independently, and it emerged exclusively from the privileged class, from the nobility. The history of the world has never seen another example of such nobility of the nobility."
(Karl Marx on the Polish Constitution of May 3, 1791)

"...the productivity of the younger part of our workforce is declining relative to the level of productivity achieved by the retiring baby boomers. This raises some major concerns about the productive skills of our future U.S. labor force."
 (Alan Greenspan 2011)

Chapter 15 - Responsible Corporations

I headed this chapter with two different quotes. First, Karl Marx on the nobility of the nobility and second, Alan Greenspan on the productivity of youth. We will get back to Greenspan later.

Nobility of the Nobility

Karl Marx was not a fool. Perhaps he had too high an opinion of the nature of man, and man's ability to work cooperatively, communally, and with a full regard for the welfare of his brother. Marx' conceptual sharp division of society into the bourgeoisie and proletariat was based on the huge divide in wealth and access to resources enjoyed by the rich capitalist class, and the exploitation and poverty of the lower working class of the 19th century.

Born into an upper middle class family, he attended both the University of Bonn and the University of Berlin, and was a historian, journalist, sociologist, and economist – more renaissance man than fool. He died in 1883.

Had he somehow been transported from the 1860s into the U.S. in the 1960s, my reading of the man is that he would have been **pleased** to see the progress in reducing the wealth gap, in the elimination of most of the crushing poverty of his own times, in the ability of workers and management to negotiate and work together to solve problems, and in the structural and economic conditions that resulted.

He would have been less keen to see the continued gap between white and black, having penned a congratulatory letter to Abraham Lincoln and the American people in 1864, commending them for their actions in putting an end to slavery.

But he would have been **equally disappointed** if he had visited Russia – the communist heartland, for he would have seen that the world that he and Engels envisioned did not turn out quite the way they had planned.

But believing, as he did, in the irreversible if gradual evolution of mankind into an egalitarian society, he would have been flabbergasted to visit again in 2012! WTF? What happened to the Nobility in the U.S., and of the U.S? What happened to this beacon of freedom, this land where all men are created equal, and with equal opportunity?

What happened to the Nobility of U.S. Capitalists – like Henry Ford, Hewlett and Packard, the Wright Brothers, Howard Hughes – the inventors and visionaries, who set out to build enduring companies and advanced products – all "Proudly Made in America"? And built the largest and most productive middle class in the world?

The Economic Time Bomb

The answer is greed, and Milton Friedman. In his watershed 1970's work on the Social Responsibility of Business, Friedman lays out the tenants of the theory which is most often rendered simply as: "The corporation's only responsibility is to make profits for the shareholders".

("The Social Responsibility of Business is to Increase its Profits", by Milton Friedman, The New York Times Magazine, September 13, 1970.)

Now in fairness to Friedman, he put some caveats in that paper, but these caveats seem remarkably easy to ignore, and clearly have been ignored in the rush to maximize profits. Maybe people get tired and fall asleep before they get to the last line of his essay, which ends:

> "...so long as it stays within the rules of the game, which is to say, engages in open and free competition without deception or fraud."

No cartels, no shill game, no shell game, no steal game. Wow! Like that happened!

Once we accept the premise that profits are all that matters, the conditions are set to begin the massive transfer of wealth, away from the middle class, and end-running the Nobility, who actually like making stuff. Only five years after Friedman untied the knot of ethics that created something of an American social compact between Capital and labor, Sam Walton was in China.

The fuse is set. It is just a matter of time because Friedman has also ignored the effects of Globalization and the huge disparity in regulations, labor costs, and labor standards around the world. It seems he lived in that ivory tower, plunked down inside the box of U.S centric thinking.

Let's play the TV game show, **"What's in the box?!?!"** Would our "girl next door" please reveal the first box puzzle. O.K! Here we go:

- Imagine that you have a box, and inside that box you have capital, labor, and raw materials.
- The capital is used to build factories and machines, and the labor takes the raw materials and adds value to it by producing stuff.

- Some of that produced stuff is circulated in the box, and some is shipped out of the box in exchange for more capital.

For $16,000 dollars, your question is:

At the end of one year, is there:
- (a) more capital
- (b) less capital
- (c) the same amount of capital

- in the box?"

"I'll go with 'a'."

"Yes, the contestant has $16,000 dollars! Do you want to keep the money, or keep on playing? Ok, so our beautiful long-legged assistant in the short skirt will reveal the next box puzzle. And here it is!:

- Imagine that you have a box, and inside that box you have capital, labor, and raw materials.
- The capital is used to build factories and machines, and the labor takes the raw materials and adds value to it by producing stuff.
- All of that produced stuff is circulated in the box, but some of the capital is shipped out of the box in exchange for more stuff.

For $32,000, your question is:

At the end of one year, is there:
- (a) more capital
- (b) less capital
- (c) the same amount of capital

- in the box? No hints from the audience now."

"Let me think.... I guess I'll go with 'b'."

144

"Yes! The contestant has thirty-two thousand dollars. Do you want to keep the money, or keep on playing? Ok, so here is the last box puzzle. These are getting more difficult now, so keep your wits about you. Ready?

- Imagine that you have a box, and inside that box you have capital, people, and raw materials.
- The capital is used to buy up factories and machines, scrap them or ship them out of the box, along with a good part of the raw materials, patents, know how, etc.
- The capital generated by these sales is generated **outside** the box, and rather than being put back in the box, it is put in a bunch of smaller boxes in scattered locations around the world.
- Not much of anything is now actually produced in the box, but the people in the box still need stuff, so more capital flows out of the box in exchange for more stuff the people actually need: food, clothes, Ipods, that kind of thing.

For $64,000, and take your time on this one:

If this process is continued year after year, what will be the end result? Is there:
(a) more capital
(b) less capital
(c) the same amount of capital
(d) no capital at all

- in the box?"

Welcome to the reality of the economic time bomb!

If we could win $64,000 that easily, we would all quit our jobs (assuming we still have jobs) in order to go full time on game shows. In fact, I wonder sometimes if that is not where we are headed.

But of course once enough of the capital has disappeared from the box, product placement shows will lose their appeal, because no one will have the money to buy stuff.

In fact, I notice an increasing focus in business rags these days on how fast the middle class is growing in Asia. They are the next big market. *Why bother wasting time on the shrinking middle class in the U.S? They are dead meat. It's just a matter of time. Let's focus on selling in China.*

Maybe that is why there is so much of a shift in prime time from product placement shows to "reality TV", where we hold up the mirror to today's society, brought to you by "The Maggots and Tapeworms of America Inc."

Look at the message. Pure end-game capitalism. There can be only one winner. So everyone else has to lose. Make it about survival. Only the fittest survive, Darwinian like. Get contestants to collude, lie, cheat, split into factions. As the numbers of survivors goes lower, the going gets tougher.

But I digress (again). Bad habit in writing. (Mental note to self – plan another book. That way you can file some of the more outrageous stuff for later!)

Back to the boxes. No one needs to be a rocket scientist to figure out what was happening here, and no one needs to be a rocket scientist to figure out the logical end-game result if you have the situation described in the final question.

And no one needs to be a rocket scientist to recognize that the third box is a simple model of the U.S. economy, 2012 version, compared to the first box around lets say 1950.

If I give you the hint "Walmart", you can probably figure out the time line for box two. So no matter what the spin of the tapeworms and maggots, this simple model explains where the U.S. was, and where it is going. There is a train wreck looming ahead, and too many people are asleep at the switch.

The U.S. is not the only economy in the Western World with this problem – just the biggest, at least in dollar terms. Just to the North of the U.S., there is a physically even bigger box, but with far fewer people. That leaves a lot more room for resources in the box, so let's talk about resources.

If you have a box with lots of resources (raw materials) and people (labor) and capital, you can build stuff, and you can sell stuff. When the resource level is super high, and the population low, one way to bring in capital is to sell extra resources. So the Canadian box was very much this model for many years. And we became moderately prosperous, much like our neighbors to the South. Countries like Saudi Arabia and Kuwait also played this game, becoming very well off on a per capita basis.
.

In the past, the resource game worked pretty well for these countries, Canada included. But there were lots of countries out there, in Africa in particular, and in other places like China at the turn of the 20th century, where the game did not work quite the same as it played out in Canada or Kuwait. What was different? Availability of capital and who owned it.

"Could we have a new contestant please. Yes, and could you tell us your name please?"

"Stephen? Well Stephen, welcome to tonight's addition of **"The Box Game!"** So let's play "What's In The Box?!?!" Would our lovely Helena please reveal the first box puzzle. O.K! Here we go:

- Imagine that you have a box, and inside that box you have labor, and lots of raw materials, but not really large amounts of capital.
- Somebody outside the box offers to buy the raw materials, and to use local labor at modest to low wages to get them out of the ground, **but -**
- The rules are that the raw materials must then be shipped out of the box. The raw materials cannot be processed inside the box.

- Once out of the box, more capital and labor will be used to add value to the resources by producing stuff, but that will be outside of the box. Some of the finished stuff might be sold back to the people in the box, naturally for more money than the raw materials fetched, since value has been added.

Now Stephen, this one is **really** tricky because there are **two** correct answers. Are you ready?

O.K. For $16,000 dollars, your question is:

What is this box an example of?
    (a) The U.S. prior to 1776
    (b) Home of a Prime Minister dedicated to the welfare of his country
    (c) A prosperous and sustainable economy
    (d) A colony

"What was that... say again? Ohhhh – Stephen! I'm so sorry! No, (b) and (c) are not correct. The correct answers are (a) and (d). So I guess you will be leaving the show and not returning next week *{aside to audience with a wink and a nod "or ever we hope!"}*. Helena, could you please show Stephen to the door."

"Could we have the next contestant please."

So when Friedman laid out his thesis of "maximizing profits", he did not seem to consider the impacts of globalization, free trade, and the easy movement of capital in a very non-homogeneous World.

He did not seem to think about how that might play out if, pressured by shareholders, or the sheer greed and hunger for power of C-level executives, corporation did not stay: "...within the rules of the game", but rather would engage in cartels, monopolies, and widespread deception and fraud.

Or what would happen if really greedy people could engage in these destructive practices with the blessing, financial support, and cheer leading of governments.

Taxes on Production vs. Taxes on Capital Gains

Let's look for a minute at some of the other factors that have been operating to mess with the system. Robert Reich has provided some figures that are of interest, specifically that the marginal tax rate under Eisenhower was 93%, dropping to 81% prior to the 1980's, to a current rate of 35%, unless we are talking capital gains, in which case the rate is 15%.

As he points out, most of the super rich make the majority of their money from so called capital gains – what Marx called the occult ability for money to add value to itself, without labor.

I am very aware of some of these effects, because the returns on interest became smaller and smaller with the plunging interest rates from their all time high in the early 80's to super low in 2008.

For anyone who had even a little bit of money as a nest egg, this meant that relying on interest to keep pace with inflation was a losing game, and the only hope of reasonable return was the stock market – assuming of course that that game was not being played with loaded dice. Meanwhile, the rate on capital gains was decreasing steadily. That was what tempted me, and what cost me a big chunk of my personal nest egg. Did that happen to you?

There is an implicit assumption in all of this, which is a fundamental tenet of capitalism and of trickle down economics, and that tenet is that the presence of capital will create enterprises and jobs, thus boosting everyone to a higher plane. So governments tax capital gains at a lower rate because that capital will create jobs and simultaneously increase taxes for all of the wage earners.

This all works hunky dory unless (1) you reach a point where fantasy finance makes creating jobs a waste of good capital, which could otherwise just add value to itself of itself, without the need to actually make anything; and/or (2) the taxation system works at a national level within a country, but the wealth generation system is global, so that one can get the tax break regardless of where the jobs are created.

In the simplest case, consider that I set up a Canadian corporation, and attract 10 investors. Since the company is a Canadian Corporation, investors in Canada get a 50-cent dollar taxation rate. If they make $100.000, they get taxed on $50,000. Now the assumption in setting this up, is that my corporation employs Canadians, who also pay taxes, so the government gets back in payroll taxes and employee income taxes an amount greater than taxes on the $50,000 dollars passed up with the capital gains tax rate.

But in this system, nothing says I have to employ Canadians, so I can actually set up my production in China, using shabby environmental laws and minimal if any worker protection, and run my "Canadian" business without any Canadian workers. But my Canadian investors and I still get the same tax break as they and I would get if the workforce were in Markham, Ontario.

In fact, I might be able to even further reduce my taxes on the business by paying business tax at a reduced rate in a foreign jurisdiction. So the Canadian tax system, and the Canadian taxpayer is actually subsidizing my outsourcing of jobs.

Is this rocket science? Should even dumber than average politicians see this as unworkable in the long term? To all appearances, they don't see any problem here, because this is essentially what is happening all around the globe.

And this is how Mitt Romney can have a 14% tax rate, while some poor smuck earning $50,000 per year pays about 35%.

The Externalised Cost Time Bomb

And then there is the piece that Friedman seems to totally leave out, unless I am misreading it – no externalization of costs. He doesn't even seem to consider this possibility at all.

What do we mean by "externalizing of costs". To increase profits, one must either increase revenues or reduce costs. That's the way a revenue-expense sheet works. Preferably you do both. The Shell game often involves taking costs off the balance sheet by transferring those costs to a Shell company, and hiding them there. But that works for only so long, before someone gets wise. And it requires breaking Friedman's maxim of "… without deception".

What if I had a "cost hole", like Orwell's "memory hole". I could just throw my costs in the "cost hole" and they would disappear from the balance sheet. Bingo, same sales, higher profits. So how can I do this? Well I just have to find a cost hole. So here are a couple of simple examples.

I'm running a mining operation for gold. To get the gold out of the ore easily, I use cyanide. It's really toxic stuff, but it is relatively cheap, and I can train my crews to handle it more or less safely. The problem is that shipping and recycling the residue after the extraction is going to be really pricey. So I need to get that cost down. So I find a cost hole. Not hard at all. Dig a hole, and pour the residue in. Done. It's off the balance sheet.

I'm running a power plant. The cheapest fuel around is coal. So let's use coal to maximize profits. Now the output from the stacks is rather yeuchy, but there's lots of space up there in the sky, so let's just pour it out of the stacks into this cost hole in the sky. Done. It's off the balance sheet.

You're ahead of me, right? The problem with these cost holes is that somebody else inevitably picks up the tab. When the cyanide leaks into a stream, or into the groundwater, people and/or other animals die. The coal ash causes literally thousands to contract cancer, asthma, emphysema and other diseases. But hey, I'm all right Jack. Those are not on **my** balance sheet.

That's externalizing costs. Get 'em off my balance sheet, and onto somebody else's balance sheet, preferably of a group who are less able to protect itself, such as poor neighborhoods, or aboriginal reserves, or the taxpayer. The time bomb is ticking.

Well, how about focusing on the revenue side, rather than externalizing costs? I make cigarettes. Sales are good. People like the product; in fact they get completely hooked on it! What if I could hook them easier, and for longer, and get them to use more? Could I increase the addictive component to a higher level? I'll just call the guys down in the lab:

"Hey John, do you think you could actually make our cigarettes more addictive? Swell, just swell."

(Ring!) "Yes Mary? ……What? You mean they actually figured out that these things cause lung cancer? Damn! **Well deny it!** *Mobilize the whole marketing department if you have to. Get that lab that we fund over at the university to make a statement to the press, and get a written response out – fast! Dr. Twerp is really good with number and statistics. Get a copy of that damned research, and tell Twerp to figure out how to debunk it. Yeah! And make sure he* **understands** *his next grant depends on his showing this new research is rubbish!"*

And we know this Worm Monologue is pretty much descriptive of how that particular scenario played out. In fact, Dr Robert N Proctor, from the History Department of Stanford University, states that the link between the epidemic of lung cancer and cigarettes was recognized in the 1940's and 50's. Yet by 1960, only one-third of U.S. doctors believed the case against cigarettes had been established. The industry knew years before, and covered it up. But no one went to jail.

Cigarettes are still legal. They cause about 1.5 million deaths a year, and the number is going up. Based on the number of deaths divided into the profits, Proctor calculated that the value of a life to a cigarette maker is about $10,000. Life is cheap.

Meanwhile, the National Institute of Health calculates that treatment of lung cancer in 2010 cost $12 Billion, which naturally the government or your private insurers are covering. That is externalized cost.

The healthcare and environmental costs keep climbing. That is an externalized cost time bomb.

The Unethical vs. the Illegal Conundrum

So here we have the conundrum. Cigarettes are legal, but they kill. The manufactures and the shareholder know that they kill. The government knows they kill. Both know that the costs are externalized, born by the Government or the private insurance industry – which means that you are paying the bills. But if someone has to die so the corporation can book $10,000 in profit, so be it. Buyer beware.

And they have been getting away with this for decades. How can they be so unethical? So amoral? Remember that conversation that Andrew Harvey had in Rio?

> "I know exactly what my company is doing, and the devastation it is causing to thousands of lives…. I know, and I do not care."

> "I know too that none of my shareholders care a rat's ass what I do, or how I do it, providing I keep them swimming in cash" (The Hope, p 174)

Do you work for a tobacco company? Do you sell tobacco in your corner store? Do you grow tobacco? Is shipping tobacco products a substantial part of your business? Do you advertise for tobacco companies?

Do you smoke on the set because the character would have smoked? Being a James Bond fan, and having watched every one of the Bond movies, I am always struck by the fact that Sean Connery's Bond smoked like a chimney.

Product placement? You betcha. A nifty way to circumvent advertising laws. Yep.

Meanwhile, according to the Center for Disease Control website:

> "More deaths are caused each year by tobacco use than by all deaths from human immunodeficiency virus (HIV), illegal drug use, alcohol use, motor vehicle injuries, suicides, and murders combined."

Are you a shareholder in a tobacco company? Is your pension fund invested in tobacco companies? Do you even know?

In a listing of the top 25 most profitable tobacco companies are the ones we all know and love, companies like Imperial Tobacco Group, Philip Morris International, British American Tobacco, who are either associated from the past with the industry, or at least are honest enough to still have Tobacco in their name, which is a bit of a giveaway.

But how about companies like Carrefour Property Development SA, who are the 6th most profitable tobacco company? Or Ceylon Grain Elevators PLC., Ceylon Guardian Investment Trust PLC, Ceylon Leather Products PLC, Ceylon Tea Brokers Ltd., Ceylon Tea Services PLC, Ceylon Theatres PLC? According to the www.ranker.com website, these innocent sounding companies come in at numbers 7 through 12 on the profitable tobacco business scale.

Here's a good one for you, number 23, Philippines Savings Bank. Do you "care a rat's ass?"

Now in fairness to the tobacco industry, I should point out that the "rat's ass" comment did not come from the tobacco industry – it came from the Genetically Modified Foods industry. But of course GMOs are perfectly safe. The industry tells us that all the time. They have studies. They are FDA approved. Fewer than one-third of U.S. doctors believe the case against ~~cigarettes~~ genetically modified foods has been established.

Truth in advertising. I made that last statistic up, just for the effect. If I had to guess based on what I read, in North America it is probably fewer than 1 in ten, rather than 1 in three.

Do your own test – ask your doctor(s). Ask them if they have personally studied the research. Hint: They don't have time, really they don't! They don't even have time to look at the research on drugs. Ask them. "When did you last read an independent study of drug efficacy, to check out how it compares against the monograph from the pharmaceutical company?" Then ask them why GMOs foods are banned for human consumption in Europe.

Monologue: *"Those weenies in Europe that don't allow GMOs to be sold for human consumption? They're just jealous 'cause they don't have the patent."*

That study released in Europe in September 2012, showing vastly different cancer rates in rats eating GMO foods and exposed to low-level Round-up residues? *Dr. Twerp was on that one in a flash. His funding is assured for another year.*

Meanwhile, three of the biggest food corporations in the U.S. – household names all – help fund campaigns to try to stop passage of Proposition 37 in California, which would make GMO labeling mandatory. *"What y'all don't know won't hurt ya!"*

Just like what you don't understand about these CDOs and CDSs won't hurt you – much! I mean, what's a few trillion among friends? Cumon…..

Yellow Sticky Note: Root problem – Immoral Owners and C-level execs who know their products are toxic and REALLY don't care.

Blue Sticky Note: Proposed solution – Put the bastards in jail. Charge them with murder. If the case is not really watertight that they knew the full extent of the damage – plea bargain criminal negligence causing death. Lock them up with the political tapeworms. Confiscate all of their assets, including their Swiss Bank Accounts, cars and yachts, and the mansions that house their trophy wives.

My Notes for the Team Meeting: Is that last one fair? What did the poor wife do? Look, she either knows what is going on, or she is a total Bimbo. That's pretty much the choice.

Yellow Sticky Note: Root problem – The state religion of money worship.

Blue Sticky Note: Proposed solution – we all need to stop worshipping money, ours or anyone else's. It is just a medium of exchange for labor.

My Notes for the Team Meeting: If someone has a lot of money, let's not get all in a tizzy. Did he or she come by this through honest hard work and/or real inventive smarts? Or is he or she a tapeworm? Why would you want to associate with a tapeworm? Why would you want to be in the same room with a maggot that lives off other people's flesh.

Remember Nick Leeson, the rogue trader that gambled big, hid his loses, and eventually brought down Barings Bank, triggering all kinds of collateral damage. Would you feel it was a source of pride to have some item of his clothing, like he was a rock star or something?

That seems genuinely "icky" to me. But his "trading jacket", the jacket he purportedly wore on the trading floor when doing his deeds, sold at an auction for £21,000. Now it did have stripes, which was perhaps prophetic. You can find pictures and description on the web – naturally.

If I went into Paul's mansion and Paul dragged it out proudly, I would have difficulty not gagging. In the highly unlikely event that Paul happens to read this, I have some advice. Find a homeless person and give it away. But please don't tell that person where it came from. Most homeless people would have too much pride to wear it, if they knew the history.

And Paul could, I have reason to believe, afford to just give it away to a street person. In 2006, his Three Delta Fund, backed by money from Qatar, bought the Four Seasons healthcare group for £1.4 Billion. I'm sure his commissions on that would keep him in beans for a while. £21,000 for Leeson's jacket is not even a blip.

Now being a curious sort, and having stumbled across Leeson's jacket, and then the jacket buyer, Paul, I also found the acquisition activity. So on some kind of weird hunch, I checked out Four Seasons. The company is in the long-term-care-homes business – a growing market given our aging demographic – providing housing for grannies.

By 2009 – just three years later, Four Season's was in deep doo-doo, and in negotiations to halve its £1.5bn debt – so by my "back of the envelope" calculations, that means someone would be out £750 Million. So there would have to be lots of losers here. But there were £600 Million in bonds that originated the leveraged buyout. Are you ahead of me on this? Yep! The Secured Creditors Game. That Qatari backed fund does not lose a cent.

Instead, The Royal Bank of Scotland was set to become the largest shareholder. That would be the same Royal Bank of Scotland that was part of the LIBOR scandal 3 years later in 2012.

So now these fine upstanding bankers who play fast and loose with the interest rates are the majority shareholders in a business, which, if it goes further wrong, will put peoples' grannies in the street. Does that give you confidence?

The CEO of Four Seasons Health Care, describing the difficulties of the negotiations and difficulty of carrying on the day-to-day business of keeping grannies off the streets, said:

"One of the most difficult issues was how to manage the business when there was highly speculative and mostly misleading information doing the rounds."

("Four Seasons finally restructured", Anousha Sakoui, Financial Times {www.ft.com} October 9, 2009.)

Shill games, shell games, someone-take-the-fall games.

Yellow Sticky Note: Root problem – The public is not demanding the truth and not demanding accountability.

Blue Sticky Note: Proposed solution – Pay attention. Do our own research into the research. And into who is paying for the research. When something really, really stupid shows up, like the recent North Carolina law that tries to tell scientists how to do climate research, laugh at them – **publicly and loudly**. Ask questions of the press. Ask your doctor. Ask your representative.

Yellow Sticky Note: Root problem – Some people are inside, see what is going on, know it is wrong, but feel trapped. Their soul is in a box.

Green Sticky Note: If you are on the inside, and you know what is happening, what should you do? This is a tough one, because whistle blowers do not always get the level of support and protection they deserve. Ask Huck Finn what he would do? Maybe hire Daniel Webster?

Blue Sticky Note: Proposed solution – At the least, get your resume out to companies that do not insist on owning your soul.

Blue Sticky Note: Proposed solution – Looking for a job? Don't apply to work for Maggots Inc.

Green Sticky Note: How long could these companies survive without complicit employees? Have there been any successful examples of employee revolt? Can employees change the culture at the top?

Yellow Sticky Note: Root problem – Some people don't give a rat's ass.

Blue Sticky Note: Proposed solution – "Out" the murder incorporated companies big time. Hammer them in the media, including the social media. Give them a broadside. When water starts to flow through the hull, the rats will scramble over the side. And the ship will sink. Keep track of where the execs go. They will try again.

Yellow Sticky Note: Root problem – Some people just don't get it. The chains are too light.

Blue Sticky Note: Proposed solution – Yes, some of your friends might need to "wake the *(bleep)* up". If they are really in deep slumber, you might need to be gentle. They might press the snooze button – maybe several times. Work on it.
[Advert: maybe you could give them a book on the topic as a present ;-)]

Too Big to Fail

One of the reasons for massive government intervention in the sub-prime crisis was the notion that banks, insurance companies, and larger manufacturing companies such as GM have become "too big to fail", meaning that the disruption to the entire economy will be so extreme that government has to step in and bail them out, which might or might not work.

In the case of banks and similar organizations, the arguments revolve around the continued availability of money for financing ongoing business. In the case of manufacturing, the concern is huge ripples in the supply chain – the hundreds of "first tier" and possibly thousands of "second tier" companies that are the suppliers to mammoth manufacturing companies such as GM.

My short term take, based on what has happened to date, is that for folks that make stuff, like GM, the lifeline can work. GM is not totally out of the woods yet, and lots of blood was let, but they appear to be headed back to profitability, and are going in the right direction. So on that one, we'll see.

As for the money folks, that is an even tougher call. People who play with money will even play with "bail-out" money. And when the board of directors of the Fed, who are doing the bailouts, includes board members who are CEOs of some of the banks on the receiving end, that looks to me like collusion and conflict of interest.

I'll leave that for someone else to follow up on – but the regulators, and the lawmakers, and the law enforcers who run homes for tapeworms, really should be looking closely at what has gone on since 2008 on this particular front.

The bottom line is that "too big to fail" is a massive problem for government and the taxpayer, and business continuity, and "too big to fail" needs to be fixed. It is interesting that the potential for the combination of investment banking and insurance firms to become "to big to fail" was actually raised by a Democrat (Dingle D-Mi) in Congress during the debate of the "Gramm-Leach-Bliley Act", but apparently no one listened.

Yellow Sticky Note: Root problem – Too big to fail.

Blue Sticky Note: Proposed solution – Put some size limitations on businesses, and accelerated business growth in a short period of time.

My Notes for the Team Meeting: Now this one is really tricky! Limitations would have to be consistent with the market space and the business type; would have to prevent creation of monopolies, by real enforcement of anti-monopoly legislation, and would have to put the brakes on risky ventures that are likely to crash and burn, and ventures that are too highly leveraged.

All of this requires government will. Absent that, bad things happen. For example, another FOG (Friend of George) by the name of Bill Gates was able to machinate the collapse of the anti-trust legislation against a big monopoly called Microsoft. Has this been good for the rest of us? Not really.

Green Sticky Note: Is the statement of the root problem too broad? Could changes in the way that executives are compensated, changes in banking regulations or behavior, or just plain old investor smarts accomplish the objective of lowing the incidence of "too big to fail" without actual legislative limits on size per se?

Green Sticky Note: How can we stabilize companies against short-term downturns so that they don't require massive government-assisted bailouts – as happened in the auto industry and banking industry – or result in huge losses for unsecured creditors and pensioners?

Green Sticky Note: Do we need to actively force divestiture so that companies that are "too big" or have monopolized large chunks of the market are forced to split up?

Too Big to be Innovative

Too big to fail is not the only consequence of super-sizing companies. It is interesting that again and again we hear that small business drives employment and drives innovation. We say it, but then we act like we don't believe it. If we did really believe it, then governments and banks would pay a lot more attention to smaller companies than they do. Are large companies really innovative? By any kind of size-versus-innovation comparison, I would say no, not from where I sit, anyway.

Do you see more and more "same old same old" around? Look at the cars in the street. If you can't see the little brand label on the back, they mostly look the same, have the same parts, work the same way …. It has been ages since a really novel solution has come along. The so-called "Smart" car is the last one I can think of, and it is rather underwhelming. Is innovation a problem in 2012, and is a part of that a result of companies getting bigger?

Since I raised the question, you might assume that I think this is the case, and you are right about that. But why would that be? It seems rather counter intuitive, because these organizations have huge research capabilities, hundreds or thousands of bright engineers – so what gives.

Very simple really – too many middle managers, too many meetings, too many agendas, too many armchair quarterbacks, too many bean counters, "paralysis by analysis" … the list goes on. Look around: there are hundreds of examples.

Don't innovate, buy!

In fact, it seems to be that big companies actually know that they are very bad at innovation. Their alternate approach is to buy out some innovative smaller company that has a competitive or "compatible" product. Unfortunately, inside the bigger company, these new product lines are often gutted, with some of the guts left to rot, while the juicier bits get smashed together with existing products to try to enhance the existing products' curb appeal.

162

Sometimes this works, sometimes it is unmitigated disaster that leaves customers in the lurch. This happens a **lot** in the software biz, a space where I have been a "power user" for over 40 years. The consequences frequently have mixed results, and often leave customers hanging. I have up-close and personal experience with an e-learning development tool from Authorware, Inc., founded in 1987 by Dr. Michael Allen, who was an expert in the field.

"Authorware" was extremely innovative, based on a simple graphical representation of the learning process, and as a result it rapidly gained 80% market share. Then in 1992, Authorware, Inc. merged with Macromind/Paracomp, who had a "sort of competitor" and "sort of complementary" product called "Director", based on a "video frame or movie frame" concept, as you might glean from the name. These were very different models, one coming from a concept-building/interactive-learning worldview, and one coming from the show-and-tell video worldview.

The resulting merged company was called Macromedia, which in turn was absorbed into Adobe Systems in 2005. Along the way, the Authorware product slowly morphed, and learned to talk to Director, and to Flash, the ubiquitous web product that can be considered to be a direct successor of Director.

An Authorware 7 release in 2003 turned out to be the last release, leaving hundreds of companies such as mine, basically high and dry. One can assume that a part of this was an ongoing struggle of worldviews, and guess that there were more than a couple of egos involved.

It is rumored that the Authorware 8 release (that never was) could directly output Flash executables, which, if true, would have competed directly with the Adobe Flash authoring system that was generating a lot of Adobe's revenue.

There are also rumors of a breakdown in communications between the Macromedia engineers in the U.S. and the development/ programming team that Adobe C-levels and bean counters, in their infinite wisdom, decided to move to Bangalore.

These Pesky Entrepreneurial Types

The "pesky entrepreneur" variation on the "don't innovate" model occurs when risk averse and/or poorly informed boards of directors deliberately force out the C-level owner/entrepreneur who was responsible for getting the ball rolling in the first place. This seems incredible on the face of it, but has happened many times.

Probably Steve Jobs is the best single example. Look it up. Really entertaining – kicked out in a power struggle in 1985, founded NeXT computer, acquired Pixar out of Lucasfilm, became the largest individual shareholder in Disney, and then ended up rescuing a near bankrupt Apple in 1997-1998, tuning them into internet tunes and sexy cell phones.

And he's not the only one. Jack Tramiel founded Commodore, and was forced out. He went on to found Atari, whose ST computer line became the rival Commodore Amiga's nemesis on the premises.

Closer to home, about 2 miles down the road from Nortel's massive research, development, and production center in Ottawa, Terry Mathews (now Sir Terry Mathews) and Michael Cowpland were effectively forced out of Mitel, a company they had founded, by directors from British Telecom, who had just purchased Mitel.

Cowpland went on to found Corel. Mathews went on to found Newbridge Networks Corporation in 1986. In 2000, he cashed out his Newbridge stock for a reputed $7 Billion, passing control of the public company to French telecom giant Alcatel.

164

How could they do it to us? Couldn't they wait a few years?

There is a flip side to this "pesky entrepreneur" gambit. Often smaller companies are founded as spin-offs of larger companies, because the larger companies cannot act on new ideas. Decision-making is too diffuse, with too many vested interests, so in frustration and self-interest the really clever engineers bail, and start their own companies.

They are not forced out – they just walk out. These spin-offs frequently do better in the marketplace, certainly from a return on capital perspective, than the unwilling parent. Of course big companies try to prevent this aberrant behavior with all kinds of nasty language in employment contracts.

I'll cover your back!

In some companies, there are actually astute C-levels who have their eye on the future and really understand their industry. If they can take a calculated risk, good things can happen. But to do this, they need a way to work around the bureaucracy, and to keep the bean counters and backstabbing machine under control. So they use a work around called "the skunk works". They might have to bamboozle the board for a bit, and just hope the results start to roll in. Don't ask for permission; ask forgiveness.

Probably the most famous example of a skunk works was the sequestering of a group of IBM employees to work on what would become the IBM PC, away from the "monster mainframe" builders and all of the bureaucracy of the massive company. Has that little innovation impacted our world?

[Two bits of interesting trivia from www.economist.com - the "skunkworks" name was based on a "moonshine factory" featured in Al Capp's wonderful cartoon series "Li'l Abner", but Lockheed Martin Corporation actually trademarked Capp's inventive name (WTF? – guess the USPTO doesn't read the comics!). Lockheed Martin provided one of the first models for skunkworks back in the 1940's – by setting up a group to fast-track design of an aircraft that would outperform the Messerschmitt BF-109.]

Yellow Sticky Note: Root problem – Most big companies are not innovative, quite the opposite.

Blue Sticky Note: Proposed solution – Shed the "bigger is better" mind set.

Green Sticky Note: Are there serious problems in the boards of directors in large firms? The upper management?

My Notes for the Team Meeting: I personally get really, really nervous when companies that I have invested in start increasing the number of lawyers, accountants, and funds managers on the board of directors, and decreasing the number of people who actually have a good understanding of the business the company is in. It seldom, if ever, seems to turn out that well. And you already know my thoughts on C-levels who manage-by-the-numbers and have a very limited understanding of the business.

Green Sticky Note: Are there better business models that we could use? If bigger is not better, how can we deal with organic growth? What can we learn from the stories of Job's, Tramiel, and Mathews?

My Notes for the Team Meeting: I am far from an expert in this space, which is why we need a team approach. But our company did work directly with both Newbridge and Mitel over the years, and through that relationship, have some understanding of how they worked, and how they differed from companies like Nortel.

[Nortel didn't like either of them very much and seemed to consider them nosy neighbors, to the extent that the Nortel reps once stormed out of a multi-company meeting we had organized to talk about training, when they found out that Newbridge folks were in the same room. This was rather annoying at the time, but in hindsight was probably a good thing.]

Mathews' model was interesting because NNC deliberately spun off more than a dozen smaller companies in a fairly short period of time.

So while Nortel built a pyramid with multiple levels of management all under one great leader, Newbridge went low-rise condo. Mathews retained a financial interest in most of the spin-offs, but each had its own senior management, own mission statement, and space to grow and play. At the same time, they were non-competitive with each other, being in slightly different market spaces, and worked cooperatively with each other.

Employees, at least early on, nearly all owned some stock – they were part owners, so all capitalists. Absent the smothering corporate bureaucracy and rarified air of the upper levels of the pyramid, they were also very innovative. And most of these companies survived the tech crash of 2002. They were battered, but nothing like the debacle at Nortel.

Killing Innovation and Competition

In the absolute worst-case scenario, large companies buy out competing patents, competing technologies, or competing information sources and "bury" them, in order to protect inferior products from competition by smaller but brighter players, or for other reasons not in the public interest. This has been shown to work. I call it the "buy and bury" game.

Often the seller is just be too under capitalized to get to market himself, and he might be seduced into thinking that the larger company will run with his great idea, and he will get the royalties. Before the ink is dry on the contract, he has probably figured out that is not quite the grand plan!

For an example of this kind of scenario, go on the web and search out the history of the electric automobile and electric trams and railways, and the involvement of Big Oil at the very start of the twentieth century.

By killing the electric car, and simultaneously slowing advanced battery research, conditions were set up for the use, and eventually the over-use of fossil fuels, resulting in oil wars, pollution, and climate change. Would it have made a difference if the electric toys had been taken out of the toy box earlier?

Make the competition illegal

A variant of this gambit involves getting the government to buy into suppressing the competition. *Want to use a competitive product to get a buzz, rather than buying beer from me? We have reserved rooms for 41,000 of you, at government expense. No, it is not at a timeshare, but you will do time.* Now I'm kidding, right? Actually not.

My research says that one of the biggest lobbying pushes for the criminalization of marijuana came from a beer company executive who thought marijuana use would cut into his beer profits. Do a web search on beer and marijuana, to see how this is still playing out today. *"Hey, if we can use the government to suppress our competition, we can externalize cost, keep our market, and save on advertising. Good deal."*

A third variant is buy and bury bad news. GMO food giant Monsanto recently purchased one of the (formerly) independent companies that were in the forefront of testing GMO food products for safety. Does this pose a threat?

I am sure there is a perfectly valid reason that they felt they should own this company, including all of the research data collected to this point. Did someone mention a "memory hole" somewhere?

Yellow Sticky Note: Root problem – Big companies deliberately kill innovation.

Blue Sticky Note: Proposed solution – Stop the "buy and bury" game.

Green Sticky Note: Is there a way to prevent the "buy and bury" game from happening?

Green Sticky Note: Would a "use it or lose it" strategy, as suggested in the coming section on patent trolls, also work for buy and bury?

Patent Trolls

This is a bit off the Big Company path, since a Patent Troll could be two lawyers with one phone and a dumpy office, but patent trolls can have a serious negative effect on innovation, so with apologies I'll stick it in here, 'cause I don't have a better place to put it. A third way in which innovation gets stymied is when companies go down, and the Patent Trolls move in.

Patent Trolls think as follows: *"First I will buy up a bunch of patents, and then sit on them, just waiting for someone to unknowingly incorporate an idea that is even vaguely related to something in my patent portfolio. I have to be patient, and wait until they have committed themselves and are just turning profitable. Now I can move in and demand royalties!*

Even if my claim is questionable, I can tie them up in court, so that all of their current capital investment is at risk. If I time it right, they will sign on the dotted line, and pay for the rest of the product life. They are over a barrel, and I can laugh all the way to the bank. Ah-ha-ha-ha-ha."

For Patent Trolls, the financial and other risks are miniscule. All of the manufacturing and marketing risk is shifted to someone else, and they just have to sit under the bridge and collect the money. This operates like a huge clamp on the jugular of truly innovative and potentially very profitable and successful companies.

In addition to Patent Trolls, the opening up of so called business-process patents unlocked the door to all kinds of legal maneuvering by companies, which has been very good for lawyers' pocket books and very bad for innovation and for consumer choice in the marketplace. Much of the fault for this problem should be laid at the door of the US Patent and Trademark Office.

Yellow Sticky Note: Root problem – Innovation killers.

Blue Sticky Note: Proposed solution – Fix the USPO, because they often let people include methods in patents that should not be patent-able. The Blackboard vs. Desire to Learn patent dispute comes to mind.

Blue Sticky Note: Proposed solution – Fix patent law, with a very simple "use it or lose it" rule. You have (fill in the blank) years to incorporate your patent into something useful, and start building it. If instead you bury it, or sit on it past this statutory limit, it either (a) reverts to the original owner/inventor or (b) goes into the public domain or (c) if taxes supported the original development or developing company, the government can auction it off, or license it to other companies that will actually use it.

Blue Sticky Note: Award large damage claims to companies unjustly attacked by Patent Trolls or by companies whose "patents" are found to be useless. I mean LARGE damages, including both direct costs and the projected costs of lost business while legal issues prevent you getting to market, or interfere with your marketing.

The Rarefied Air Conundrum

Big companies also seem to reach a size where most of upper and much of middle management start to drink their own Kool-Aid. They become arrogant in ways that endanger their very survival. Alternately, they breed stupidity. If they are just arrogant, they occasionally get a slap on the side of the head, which keeps them in line for at least a period of time. If they are both arrogant and stupid, the companies are seldom long for this World.

The Gorilla Mental Muscle

The Gorillas in the market place often try to set the agenda for everyone, assuming their sheer size will carry the day. And sometimes an alliance of substantially smaller companies says "no thanks", and outmaneuvers the Gorilla.

Just ask Sony about the "Sony Beta" vs. "VHS" consumer video format wars, for example. In this particular case, Sony might rightly argue that Beta was a marginally better format than VHS, but in continuous improvement lingo, the "voice of the customer" told a different story in the long run.

Sony might be suffering through this again, as their heavy, expensive, and potentially eye-fatiguing 3D "active glasses" design competes head on with a simpler, cheaper, and more consumer friendly design from Korean manufacturer LG, teamed with a consortium of other smaller manufacturers.

One wonders if Sony was actually listening to "the voice of the customer", or were they recycling a failed product from another market (computer games?), hoping it would catch on in the even larger market (TV) – given sufficient market hype.

The Arrogance Gene

Some folks think that pyramids have all kinds of special energy focusing power, and some very interesting suggestions have been made about how pyramids could be used to help parts of the anatomy grow. Certainly when they get large enough, some type of bacteria seems to breed and grow that spreads the arrogance gene. This mostly seems to happen higher up in the pyramid.

We had some direct experience. It involved that same local company Nortel, who has already figured in this narrative. Nortel had an ESD control problem. If you know what ESD is, great. If you don't, suffice it to say Electrostatic Discharge is not a good thing if you make electronics that are supposed to be reliable in the field and cost effective to produce.

So Nortel had this problem. But some (not all) of their middle management said, "No we don't. Everything is swell, just swell. It is all under control." Not. We knew better. I had been inside the plant myself, and knew people that worked in the plant. Knowing some of the procedures, and knowing the ESD Control knowledge level of some of the people in production was kinda scary.

Some time later my wife was discussing this "all under control" thing with a recent ex-Nortel middle management "grad". (There were quite a few ex-Nortel people floating around at networking sessions by this point.) His response went something like this: "Who are you kidding? Last quarter alone, ESD damage cost them $600,000 dollars!"

That's just a part of it. One of the blood losses that they suffered resulted when they could not meet delivery of a new product, and lost a big supply contract as a result. I have had various opinions as to whether the problem in that particular case had to do with bad procedure or over promising. In either case, the result was definitely not good.

Later, when Nortel was already in its death throes, one manager got a quote from us for ESD training to arrest an immediate problem. We gave them a $5000 quote – which was a bargain, given the need. He had to have the $5000 approved by a VP! In another location! You are ahead of me on this again, right?

Yellow Sticky Note: Root problem – Big companies miss warning signs of rough water ahead and ignore advice from outsiders.

Blue Sticky Note: Proposed solution – Be on the lookout for the deviant "arrogance" gene.

Green Sticky Note: Could we develop internal or external detectors for the "arrogance" gene? Confidential customer and supplier questionnaires, for example? If we find a few people with the arrogance gene, how do we deal with it? What if it is an epidemic? What if it is at the very top? What if they are asking to borrow money, or offering to sell shares of stock or bonds?

Brain death

Another example. This was ESD control – again. Company was in the U.S. Losses were only $250,000 a quarter. Chump change. Our mid-level contact in the company figured our training could fix a lot of the problem, more or less permanently, for $25,000 – one tenth of what it was costing them every quarter. So his budget request was floated up into the rarified air, and the answer came back from the financial wizards who lived up there. "No."

Based on a 10X multiplier of benefit to cost, in just one quarter, this seems a bit strange, wouldn't you think? Well, no, apparently not. The financial wizards noted that the $250,000 in cost through ESD damage could be written off against taxes, but presumably the $25,000 would have to be amortized over several years.

Definitely a clear diagnosis of "brain dead". Lack of oxygen in the upper regions of the pyramid.

Yellow Sticky Note: Root problem – Brain death from exposure to the rarified air near the top of the management pyramid.

Blue Sticky Note: Proposed solution – Don't build the pyramid so high.

Notes: (Yellow: root cause; Blue: proposed solution; Green: question or additional data we need)

_____

_____

_____

_____

_____

_____

_____

_____

_____

_____

_____

_____

_____

_____

Chapter 16 - Inchworms and Tapeworms

We humans, the first species to combine tool using with advanced language and its attendant consciousness, were handed a "Garden of Eden". Whether your or my belief system and worldview consider this a literal or a figurative description really doesn't matter.

What matters is that at any time and in any of the smallest decisions, we have a choice point. We can choose to try to make this a better world than we found it, or we can be hedonistic. We can be an inchworm or a tapeworm - that is pretty much the choice.

If you have never watched an inchworm, take a minute from your busy day to do so. There are videos on YouTube. The inchworm progresses by first anchoring his back legs on something solid and then stretching or reaching as far as he can for a new anchor point. Sometimes it takes a moment to find, but he does generally succeed if he persists.

For us to survive as a species, we all need to anchor our back legs on something solid and then stretch. And we are going to have to accomplish it inch by inch.

If you watch one of these little guys hit a dead end and reach for the sky, there is a certain symbolic beauty in that. He will eventually turn around and try a different path, and we will have to do this on occasion too. But there is no harm in sometimes reaching for the sky. It sure beats swimming in the cesspool with the tapeworms.

So to climb back out of the abyss that we are falling into, we will need a lot of inchworms moving a little ways forward at a time, sometimes having to retrace steps, but always reaching for the sky. So I will describe some inchworms and some of the small steps we can and must take.

Boycotts and Bugging

I read awhile back of an enterprising inchworm who was writing an app so you could check if something you were thinking of buying was made by any company owned by the Koch brothers.

I think this is brilliant. I think we could have an entire family of these, and generically call them de-worming apps. A big part of having choice is having information. Boycotts of products made by companies that grossly abuse the public trust, or are owned or managed by tapeworms, is really the first step to curbing the really atrocious behavior of companies and company executives.

In addition to apps such as the one described above, we also have to get over our reluctance to say stuff to strangers. For example, I passed by the usual gianormous pile of coke in a store the other day and casually mentioned that I have not bought any coke recently. Not since I read that the company poured money into trying to block California proposition 37, which would have require labeling of GMO food.

I also alert the store manager or submit feedback forms concerning both the items I won't buy and my pleasure to find increased representation of non-GMO, Fair Trade, and other healthier and socially responsible choices. What if they heard this 5 times a day? Fifty times a day? If one large chain store stopped stocking socially irresponsible products because customers were not buying and were complaining about the company being a part of the problem, rather than a part of the solution, do you think the message would reach that company? Of course the first reaction will be spin. That is what marketing departments are for. So we need to be persistent – one inch at a time.

If thousands of consumers of gasoline in the US and Canada said to Shell: "Enough, already! Stop destruction and exploitation in Nigeria, clean up the pollution in the Delta, pay compensation to the people you have hurt, directly build schools and infrastructure using local resources, stop paying off the politicos in Lagos – do you think Shell might clean up their act?" They might have to cut back their advertising spend on TV by 10% or so to accomplish those socially constructive things and still maintain competitive pricing.

There are hundreds of cases around the world where this kind of economic colonialism operates with impunity, destroying lives and further corrupting local officials. If we work at it, using petitions and social media, we can, in effect, "outspend" companies by contributing our time to comments, blogs, postings, and petitions.

We also have to be ever vigilant of the Trojan Horse called "Free trade", and insist on "Fair trade". The problems are typified by the current situation in Canada around FIPA, and the incredibly dangerous Trans Pacific Partnership – which the independent Council of Canadians calls a "trap" – and which is raising eyebrows if not full scale rebellion south of the border as a consequence of the secrecy and lack of public and political oversight in the drafts.

So this is a dual strategy I call B&B – boycott and bug. There are hundreds of millions of us. They depend on us not paying attention, or not caring "a rat's ass" when we do catch them out of line. We can tune out and focus on bread and circuses, or we can spend some time doing our own small part to change the way the world works.

Increasingly there are groups of people and organizations that are seeing where we are heading and showing up to be counted. On the petition side, Care2Action and Avazz are the largest and most active. Avazz now has over 15 million petitioners Worldwide, and continues to grow daily. That is a lot of inchworms.

Professional groups are starting to see what is happening as well. Recently I was introduced to a group of professional engineers who are part of a movement called "Take Back Manufacturing". They see our government policies in Canada heading in the same direction as those in the U.S., and want to stop the hemorrhaging before we are in quite as big a mess.

Young people are also getting wise to some of this. I read a lament today in a university student publication that their University planned to award an honorary degree to a tapeworm. This is very common practice today. After all, tapeworms fund universities big time. There are lots of "Dr. Twerps" out there – and since far too many universities have adopted the business and profit model, and swung increasingly away from research "just because" – universities largely give these honors to those who buy them. Which brings me to the education biz.

The Colleges and Universities Biz

We have two quotes throughout this book that basically blame our problems on kids and education: Cooley, who says we are not doing enough and we need more people in Universities, and Greenspan who blames declining productivity on the young people of today. We also hear frequently that we have higher levels of debt than ever before and need to learn self-control and better money management.

Cooley's reasoning has already been questioned. But I am sure Greenspan is correct. Young people with college degrees flipping burgers, clerking in retail, or holding signs on Wall Street really aren't nearly as productive as the retiring boomers. What has changed? A whole bunch of things.

Post WWII the GI-bill and Marshall Plan had graduates pouring out of training programs and factories humming. Parents who lived through the dirty thirties understood hard work, and understood there was no dishonor in building cars and washing machines. On the consumer side, these same parents were used to living within their means.

178

And the advertising world had not yet spun totally out of control. I vividly remember our first TV (although the color was not so vivid – being limited to two – black and white). But what was so remarkably different was not the technology but how it was used, and the rules that applied.

For every 30-minute slot of programming, advertisers got three minutes! It was actually hard to get to the fridge and back without missing actual programming. (Maybe that is part of the obesity problem – long and frequent ads. That's a new thought! Put that on the "healthy living" value stream map.)

All of this was well before a really innovative entrepreneur figured out how to build a personal computer that could make a ton of money retailing at about $1000. But with new "talent" at the C-level, and a Board of Directors with "classical" business smarts, and by spending a mere million dollars in one of the most high profile TV ads of all time, this new computer came on the market at 2.5 times its design price, still sold like crazy, and the rest is history.

Consumerism is all about the advertising, which feeds into everything from buying lipstick to buying the Presidency of the United States. And consumerism drives Colleges and Universities. So if little Johnny does not get a real moneymaking degree, and become a lawyer or a brain surgeon, he is pretty much a nobody.

Universities have big bucks to help sell this message. And like the personal computer that cost 2.5 times what is was designed to sell for, universities and colleges charge an arm an a leg for the most basic of education, forget what it costs to become a lawyer or brain surgeon.

So unless your parents birthed you with the silver spoon in your mouth, you have to go to the banks for funding to get a "reasonable" education, and run up huge loans that cripple your finances before you are 25. You then arrive at the job station only to find the train has already left.

While attending a manufacturing trade show recently, I ran into an instructor who teaches tool and die making. This is a critical set of skills to have available if we are to have any chance of rebuilding manufacturing in this country. But he has a major problem because he needs very expensive equipment for the students to hone their skills.

He indicated that his program could easily place about double the number of students that he can actually turn out. But because the college is run as a business, their ROI is much higher in courses that don't need expensive equipment - just a warm body at the head of the class, preferably broadcast by closed circuit to another 10 classrooms.

So the C-level wants to cut the Tool and Die program. To keep it running, the instructor needs to personally go cap-in-hand to various equipment makers begging for resources. Meanwhile industry is complaining they can't find enough people who have the skills needed to allow them to stay competitive.

Is this in the best interest of the country? Do University and college administrators care? How much of their total funding comes from the taxpayers? What is the mission and role of education? How should it be funded and managed? How can it be made more efficient? How can Universities get back to their academic roots as seekers of truth and knowledge, and rid themselves of the Dr.Twerps and corporate funding dependence?

If you are in a less developed part of the world, you might actually have an advantage because you don't have all the high-cost and vested interests in educational infrastructure. Don't mess up by slavishly following the North American educational model. You can't afford it, don't want it, and it will not do the job for you that needs doing. Find alternative models, or pull together a team and develop your own. We need a lot of inchworms reaching for the sky on this one.

Going Public - Going Private

So capital is a problem, and people are getting very concerned. Lots of money is sidelined because people who don't have large funds to lose reach a point where they no longer trust the rules by which the market games are played. Others might hold off for any number of reasons, including both uncertainty and also in an attempt to manipulate either the market, or politics, or both.

Given the virtual disappearance of large amounts of venture capital, recently there has been a big hurrah being raised for something called "crowd funding", something that is in Obama's Job's Act, and which is being pushed heavily in Canada by some organizations.

This might be the greatest thing since sliced bread, and it might just be another way to get around the few regulations that are left to "sort-of" protect investors. The potential for fraud is huge. Who is going to participate in crowdfunding? Not the high rollers with billions in the bank. No, it will be the ever-diminishing middle class, trying to bail out the ark with teaspoons.

I would probably be more supportive of the notion if I did not recognize the uniforms worn by some of the folks who are spreading the fertilizer – at least here in Canada. At this point, it is "buyer beware", which has not proved to be a great formula for protecting us in the past.

For some time, a key component of "exit strategy" has been going public. This is where you, the originator of the great idea, cash in your chips for a big payout, and move on to bigger and better things, while "real" businessmen come in to run the current enterprise for maximum profit. It seems that all too often somewhere down the road things go off the track.

The whole notion of "exit strategy" when framed this way, seems really out of whack. I mean really, how many brilliant hits can one entrepreneur come up with? Steve Jobs, who was just a tad exceptional, came up with three or four game changers, from the Apple II in the '70s to the Ipod lineup first released in 2001. He might have the record, I don't really know.

But he did not exit Apple as a young man to cash out and go live in the Bahamas. He was forced out in a board-level power play. If you are under retirement age (whatever that actually is), going public can lead to giving up your baby for adoption to some really, really bad foster parents. And mostly to make the pyramid bigger, not necessarily better.

The rules of business financing are stacked against start-up companies, however, with "vulture" capitalists seeming to outbreed venture capitalists and angels by a substantial margin. Having participated in The Alternative Board with senior management-owner-inventor types of two different companies that were acquired by larger pyramid-building cultures, I have a rather jaundiced view of the "goings on" that can accompany this particular gambit.

There is another model, which is the well-structured and moderately funded private company, where control stays with the founders. I have some experience with two such entities, one as a youth in New Brunswick, where the family-owned Irving group of companies appears to be pretty much single-handedly responsible for keeping the economies of New Brunswick and Nova Scotia going. Without them, I think it is an open question of when the last person out would turn off the lights.

They, like all people in this kind of position, have their detractors. Are they "angels" in business? No. Have they influenced politicians? Yes. But since K.C. Irving founded the company in the 1920's, they have grown to own more than 300 companies employing thousands. One estimate that I saw suggested that Irving companies employ about 7% of New Brunswick's total workforce. K.C.'s sons and grandsons both own and run this huge conglomerate.

I met one of his sons once, when as a university student I had summer work running equipment in one of the vertically integrated side businesses that are so a hallmark of the group. (They keep their supply chain lean – by owning most of it from resource to market.) I was in early that morning in 1963, before the boss as it happened.

A young man in shirtsleeves was rifling though the boss's filing cabinets. When he noticed I was there, he came bounding out of the office, extended his hand with a big smile, and introduced himself – one of K.C.'s sons. Remember that Green Sticky Note back in chapter 12 about the CEO corner office? Remote corner offices do not seem to be the way things work in Irving-Land. The owners in this case are very hands-on.

The second example is another 2nd generation case, where I frequently discussed business issues with the owner. He took over from his father, and "organically" grew the business to rival some Gorillas in the marketplace in his particular niche. Not being beholden to shareholder groups looking for a quick buck, he has had far more room to maneuver, but to keep things boiling has also had to hold off on the "rich-and-famous lifestyle" for the sake of building his business, and securing his place in the market.

I found it an interesting study to see how much fun he was having with his product launches, and wheeling and dealing. Meanwhile, associates who were in the short term personally better off financially (because their companies had been acquired) had to suffer through the inanities perpetrated by absentee company owners who were pretty much the epitome of the absentee landowners that my GGGGrandpappy worked for centuries back.

These former owners now had to do things that they felt were questionable in terms of the long run viability of their companies because the people at the top of the pyramid were running on rarified air. So while these former owners were often critical of our "still in the driver's seat" colleague for his frugality and failure to siphon more personal money from the company, they were definitely not having as much fun as he was.

Occasionally you also see the unusual phenomena of a once public company going private. This occurs when an original owner, or someone else equally attuned to what the company is about, actually buys back most or all of the public stock and assumes controlling interest again.

This is most likely when current management, lacking the vision and direction of a founder, are sinking the company. Shares can easily fall well below the original offering price, and the founder can pick it up again for less than he sold it, and effectively remove it from both the market and the short-term market factors that drive bad business behavior.

So while privately owned companies do suffer some ups and downs, and are not isolated from the problems of a really stressed marketplace (which impacts their customer base among other things), they are also not totally twisted out of shape by shareholders and boards of directors who drive really bad behaviors for short-term profits, or at least the appearance thereof.

Society as a whole could probably get along very nicely without the existence of the mammoth, public-stock funded behemoths. Conversely, if all of the very small to mid-size privately owned businesses were to fold their tents, we would be back to the Middle Ages. It is unfortunate that governments, by and large, don't seem to recognize this, although the U.S. government actually outperforms Canada on this particular score.

The Employee Entity

How many companies have you seen trumpet on their web site that their employees are their most important asset, while acting behind the scenes or sometimes very publicly to keep the bast***s in their place? Conversely, how many employees have you seen bite the hand that feeds them? The same heightened sense of competition that seems to overtake common sense between some companies and even whole countries also divides companies internally.

This "us or them" mentality is at the core of much that holds us back. It is also a tool used by the super rich to continue to enslave us all. It is time for a "new deal" between management and labor, or management and unions – a deal founded on everyone having skin in the game and everyone being on the same side.

Postwar Japan was perhaps a good example of one set of practices that work, and these largely held together in Japan (until quite recently when some owners and managers started to emulate the greedy practices they saw in the West). It is interesting that these postwar business practices were a hard sell in the U.S., so American William Edwards Deming took his ideas to Japan.

By the time the practices began to be re-imported as a workable model in the U.S. in the 1990's, huge damage had already been done to American competitiveness – and capital was already flowing out of the box at an ever-accelerating rate.

It is an interesting fact that one of the first American auto makers to seriously look at these practices – and to hire Deming as a consultant – was Ford Motor Company in the mid 1980s. Now would that be the same Ford that was the only large auto manufacturer to refuse bailout money in 2008 because they felt they did not need it?

The concept of Lean manufacturing, as it is often called in North America, flies clearly in the face of the "managing by the numbers" taught by the top American business schools for the better part of a half century. Google "managing by the numbers" to find that managing by the numbers is either the key to "building a stronger business" or the key to "business failure … and economic disaster". Hmmm.

And the first thing that Deming did at Ford was to point directly at management practices as the key problem in achieving quality. Not a lazy, careless workforce, but management practices. And Ford listened.

I raise this issue not to promote Lean Manufacturing as a cure all (although it can help) but to point to two specific elements of the Lean philosophy that speak directly to the labor/management divide, and to the manage-by-the-numbers mentality.

First is the concept that the person or persons who are the key to improving process are the people on the floor who actually build the stuff. They generally know there are better ways to do things. But because either the culture of management is confrontational or management is particularly skilled in failing to listen to anything the workers might suggest – even viewing it as sedition – the employees shut up and do it the way it has always been done. And management sits in the office and manages by the numbers.

Second is the concept called "Gemba" in Japanese. Roughly translated this means that if you are a manager and you really want to know what is going on, go talk to the troops. Don't sit in your penthouse office reading reports written by middle managers who are primarily out to tell you what you want to hear. Unless, as we said earlier, you really haven't a clue what these people on your payroll actually do.

But in retrospect, I would like to revise my earlier suggestion that you stay in your office in that case. It would be much more honest and fair to shareholders and the company alike to say: "OK. I am out of my depth here. I will give myself a maximum of 6 months to learn how this company really operates and what those folks on the shop floor really do, and if I can't figure it out in that much time, I will surrender my stock options, and go get a job where I understand what the hell is going on."

I realize in suggesting this that I could be directly contributing to a substantial increase in the number of job seekers, in a market that is already rather difficult, but in this particular instance it might be for the best.

For a historical perspective, go back to the Apple Computer example, and speculate on where things might have gone if Apple had not brought in an executive from the food industry to run the show. They could have just hired Alan Pottasch, who is credited as the brains behind the "Pepsi Generation" ad campaign, instead of hiring the Pepsi CEO, and saved both Steve Jobs and Apple a lot of grief.

The Union Discombobulation

The flip side of the weak management coin is the union discombobulation. Unions have played an important role, and have been a brake on the worst of worker exploitation. But they have also been their own and at times the country's worst enemy, by overstepping and trying – sometimes succeeding – in blocking all attempts to make industry more effective and efficient.

I alluded earlier to the infiltration of unions by, well, gangsters. While McCarthy was searching for all those commies under the bed, it seems he was totally oblivious to the big M, which had become much bigger running booze during prohibition, and needed to find other lines of work when prohibition ended.

I lived the early years of my life in a small town with freight trains moving goods by rail close behind my house. In spite of the coal smoke that belched out of the steam engines of the time, this was actually a very energy efficient method to move large amounts of raw materials and manufactured stuff over large distances.

Thank the unions for a rapid decline in the percentage of freight carried by the railways of the nation, for increasing the death toll on the highways, for the massive increase in fossil fuel use, and for massive additional costs for highway maintenance. From an energy efficiency perspective, long haul trucking just doesn't cut it. And every time I get on the 401 out of Toronto, with a line of 18 wheelers as far as the eye can see, I am reminded how big a problem this really is.

And thanks to some years of a totally confrontational approach between automotive workers and management, many of the process improvements and automation opportunities that could have and should have been implemented in the U.S. were put on hold, weakening the American companies against foreign competition, primarily the Japanese.

To the credit of the unions, there were attempts to develop profit sharing models, but these largely went nowhere.

Yet that effort, combined with management understanding of where the value really is created, is the key to the tools that would allow us to develop a new culture, to cultivate a new approach. That might require that unions give on another major area of friction, and one that to me makes no sense – seniority.

My perspective might be colored here, because I was employed as a teacher, and as such was a member of a union, and to be quite frank, it p**sed me off that a teacher who was now a colleague, who had been a "not so hot" teacher of mine when I was a student at the school, pulled in way more money than I did, for doing a frankly inferior job, and for being the first out of the parking lot at the end of the day, while I was busy setting up for the science club or working with the student theatre group.

Seniority can do that kind of thing, and there simply has to be a better way. Unfortunately, union leadership tends to be pulled from the "seniors" in the profession, and seniority and work to rule is "word of the gospels" around these people.

Getting It Together

One way to fix some of these problems would be to make every employee a stakeholder. By that I don't mean they get to keep their job if they don't rock the boat – I mean they become "invested" in the company, either as part owners through employee stock ownership plans (ESOPs), or by participation in the profits through bonuses and similar team performance incentives.

To remove some of the risk for employees, this would require fiscal transparency in the company, and might require tax-law changes to avoid triggering unrealized gains. I'm not a tax accountant, and I am out of my depth here. I just know "unrealized gains" can be a problem.

Stock options were a key strategy for Sir Terry Mathews, as he developed and spun off the various companies from Newbridge Networks. There is a lot of money in the Ottawa area that can be traced to employment in one of these spin-offs.

It also works as a strategy in private companies. My business colleague, who was taking on the Gorillas in his market niche, set up an employee stock ownership plan with a set of rules for valuation and some degree of internal liquidity. Is this good for building employee loyalty and enhancing employee effort? You betcha.

When things go wrong

Another slant to employee ownership arises when management screws up or companies become over-extended, or companies try to get unfair concessions from workers, as happened recently in Electromotive, a Windsor, Ontario plant that manufactured railway locomotives. The ultimate owner in the U.S. had just boosted the CEO pay massively, while asking rank and file workers in Windsor to take a 50% pay cut.

When they refused, they were first locked out and then the plant was closed. It can be assumed that here, as in the Nortel case, this involved transfer of plans and patents developed with support of Canadian taxpayers to the owner in the U.S. and that those patents might well be part of their new operations setting up in China and India.

Yellow Sticky Note: Root problem – Employees and jobs take a back seat when plants close. This is lose-lose-lose for the employees, for the local suppliers, and ultimately for the economy and the government.

Blue Sticky Note: Proposed solution – Increase the employee's stake and provide Government backing when owners decide to bail. Make it much harder to buy a company, gut it, and run with the cash. Use regulations and tax law to encourage good behavior.

Green Sticky Note: What if the option, in the Electromotive case, had been that the patents and processes paid for by the taxpayer stayed with the Government? What if the employees had thought they could make a go of it, and had had the opportunity to try, with some reasonable capital backing?

Green Sticky Note: What if the government could say – Mr. Owner, you want to close this plant? OK. We have the right of first refusal on any sale of plant or equipment. Find a genuine buyer, and we will better the offer by 2%.

Green Sticky Note: What if the Government pays the workers their allocated unemployment insurance, but they stay and run the plant? When UI runs out, they are on their own. While on UI they can pay themselves a supplement up to the level of their previous wage, providing they can do so without further indebting the company.

Green Sticky Note: What if the deal includes the Government putting up a dollar in loan guarantees for every matching dollar the workforce can raise (to a negotiated limit) to provide short term operating capital?

Green Sticky Note: Are there tax tools that could discourage companies from moving production assets out of a country? I ask because it seems to me that current tax law actually encourages all of the worst practices that we have seen in the last half-century.

My Notes for the Team Meeting: We need a new compact encompassing owners, management and labor. It is in everyone's best interest. Maybe we need to discuss and agree, and look for solutions more, and "negotiate" and "litigate" less.

We also need a new social compact among all of mankind. That might take a tad longer.

Notes: (Yellow: root cause; Blue: proposed solution; Green: question or additional data we need)

_____

_____

_____

_____

_____

_____

_____

_____

_____

_____

_____

_____

_____

_____

_____

_____

_____

_____

_____

"No need for greed or hunger
A brotherhood of man"
(John Lennon, "Imagine" 1971)

"Jesus looked at him and said, "How hard it is for the rich to
enter the kingdom of God! Indeed, it is easier for a camel to go
through the eye of a needle than for someone who is rich to enter
the kingdom of God."
(Luke 18:24-25)

"But when He saves them, at once they commit injustice upon the
earth without right. O mankind, your injustice is only against
yourselves, [being merely] the enjoyment of worldly life. Then to
Us is your return, and We will inform you of what you used to
do."
(Surat Yunus - the Noble Qur'an, Sahih International 10:23)

Chapter 17 – Imagine

I wonder about those bondholders in Qatar, and about the 400 super rich people who hold American passports and who have more wealth than the bottom 150 Million other Americans taken together. I wonder why it seems so hard for them to "Imagine" a world with no need for greed or hunger. As hurricane Sandy lashes the Eastern Seaboard, leaving a trail of destruction and an initial eleven dead by the first morning, I wonder how they view their part and responsibility in committing injustice upon the earth without right.

Throughout this exploration of Capitalism and Democracy, I have put up my sticky notes to identify things that I think are problematic, and places where I think there are immediate actions that could be taken to reverse the slide into the abyss. Many of my suggestions will be very difficult to implement.

Many of my suggestions might be just plain impractical or even nutzoid, but nothing should be ruled out until you, the reader, and other members of the continuous improvement team come up with better ideas.

Bur regardless of the short term success that might be achieved through attending to these yellow and blue and green notes, it does not address the long term number one problem of unadulterated greed and pure evil.

Just as companies need vision statements and mission statements to focus their creative energy, mankind also needs a vision statement and mission statement to move forward as a species, cooperating together, just as our over fifty trillion individual cells are living entities that cooperate to make us the individuals that we are, as Bruce Lipton so elegantly explains in his works.

No child born into this world should be condemned to a short life marked by hunger and suffering. No child born into this world should be prevented and separated from the opportunity to learn and to become a functional, participating, and accepted part of the human race, no matter his or her race, his or her religion, or his or her geographic location. This is a message brought by every spiritual teacher in every religion. Why do we have such a problem in hearing and understanding this simple message?

In 2000, at the United Nations, 191 countries committed to a set of goals to be achieved by 2015. The eight goals were:

> MDG 1: eradicate extreme poverty and hunger
> MDG 3: promote gender equality and empower women
> MDG 4: reduce child mortality
> MDG 5: improve maternal health
> MDG 6: combat HIV/AIDS, malaria and other diseases
> MDG 7: ensure environmental sustainability
> MDG 8: develop a global partnership for development

How ironic that in 2000, U.S. lawmakers set loose the beast, resulting by 2012 in the U.S. in:

- Increased poverty and misery as jobs, homes, and middle class wealth disappears
- Radical right wing extremism that is actively working against gender equality and maternal health.

194

- A child mortality rate as of Jan 1, 2012 that puts the U.S. in 49th spot well behind Canada and Cuba, and 7th out of 8 in the G8 industrial nations – beating out only Russia.
- Epidemics in obesity, cancers, heart disease and growing problems such as autism and ADHD – which we treat with drugs while ignoring the root cause.
- Failure to provide global leadership in sustainability
- A turning inward and away from the rest of the world because internal problems are so pressing.

And how ironic, with the massive resources that once typified our nations, that our young people – our hope for the future, are standing on Wall Street, asking where all of the jobs are. The jobs that are supposed to magically appear, without capital or resources.

Meanwhile, Alan Greenspan in 2011, states:

"...the productivity of the younger part of our workforce is declining relative to the level of productivity achieved by the retiring baby boomers. This raises some major concerns about the productive skills of our future U.S. labor force."

Pardon me???

The Charity Chit

Jon Ronsan, in a remarkable piece of journalism for CQ.com called "The Surprising Truths About Income Inequality in America", looks at the lives and finances of five Americans who range in income from $200 per week for 27 hours spent dishwashing in a classy restaurant to $625,000 per week for a business owner who started with nothing and achieved this level by hard work, determination, and hitting on a business model at the right time in the market. Look for it on the web.

Jon's most interesting finding from the whole exercise was the range of attitudes across these multiples of income, and range of taxation, from the lowest who doesn't know how much his employer is actually deducting because he gets no accounting of this; to an investor who backed a dot com winner, pays about 11% in tax, and feels that paying 50% tax would be more appropriate; to the multibillionaire who is a substantial donor to the Republican party, is clearly very libertarian in his views, bristles about entitlement, and seems to believe that those who don't rise to the very top somehow deserve whatever misfortune befalls them.

While Jon provided the figures for the following, he did not comment on what I consider is an interesting aside; that this last extremely wealthy man went from being worth $4 Billion in 2006 to a mere $1.9 Billion in 2012. So he was massively ripped off too. Had he paid out that $2.1 Billion in tax, he would be screaming like hell.

But it is pretty safe to assume that he lost it to the shills, shells, and shorts. Is he upset about that? No, he is upset about a supposed culture of entitlement that he has been told "exists". Something that none of the other four persons interviewed for Ronsan's piece mentioned at all. Do you find this curious?

So what does this have to do with charity? A lot, in fact, because one of the ways in which the super rich, including this billionaire, feel good about themselves is that they give to charity. How frequently in the Presidential campaign of 2012 did we hear about Romney's gifts to charity? The Bill Gates foundation gives massively to charities, particularly in Africa. And Jon's billionaire gives to charities – particularly in cancer treatment and cancer research. And the Koch brothers give to charities, presumably using some of the money they made in trade with Iran.

So this is a good and a generous thing, right? Rather than giving the money to government, and letting government waste it on welfare for the "entitled", or on enforcing fair work practices and a clean environment, we the moneyed folk will decide where our hard earned money is spent.

196

Charities are band-aids, for the most part, and often do more harm than good. (Pause to duck flying tomatoes. Stop ears to block the screams of "heresy!")

How can I make such a ridiculous statement? I can because it is true. Let's look at cancer for example. My father ultimately died of cancer. He finally quit smoking after 65, and lived to 92, but it was still cancer that got him in the end. That's not what it says on the death certificate, because while fighting the lung cancer that finally caught up to him, he got a lung infection and died of "congestive heart failure", so that is what is on the death certificate.

But people still smoke. And cigarette companies still get rich. And tobacco farmers still waste the earth's resources growing this poison on land that could be producing food. And while our billionaire is giving to cancer research, millions of tons of toxic fumes continue to belch into the air, we pump toxic and cancer causing chemicals into the earth to extract more fuel for our SUVs and 18-wheelers, we contaminate our food sources with GMOs, and Dr. Twerp continues to assure us that all of this is safe.

So we put on the band-aids and ignore the root causes. And our billionaire feels good about giving to charity, and supports a party that wants to roll back control by the EPA, wants to gut environmental protections, and let the free market "work it all out". It would be funny if it were not so tragic.

We could talk about charity in Africa, at the same time as we talk about the devastation caused there to local farmers by imported food, mining pollution, factory farms, and rape of resources. Steal the resources, and give back a little charity. Ignore or even help create the conditions for tribal and religious warfare, and then send a little food aid to the refugees. Oh, and make sure that the aid is mainly spent buying food from American factory farms, and those heartland voters who help keep politics in the sorry state they are in.

Our own personal small charitable giving is primarily though micro-lending. We provide capital, in the form of tiny loans that give a small business or a single entrepreneur in the third world the opportunity to make a living. When they get their business running, the money gets re-circulated back and loaned to another. It is lack of capital and lack of education that holds back entire societies – not some inherent laziness or stupidity or sense of "entitlement" in 47% of the inhabitants.

To be very clear on this, I am not saying that all charitable giving should be stopped cold turkey. What I am saying is that depending on charity band-aids for the long haul, rather than fixing the root problems, is a dead-end street. And I have little doubt that most of the problems could be fixed, if we took the same amount of deliberation, determination, and plain old "American" ingenuity that enabled us to get to the moon and beyond.

Why doesn't this happen? Because there are a very few people who get very, very wealthy specifically because things continue in a turmoil, whether this is through selling arms or raping resources. And because pharmaceutical companies get very, very wealthy supplying drugs for what are largely preventable conditions. And because fantasy finance beats actually having to work for a living.

What if ...?

What if we changed some of the rules? What if we said, "we can all see this is not working, that things are getting worse, not better, on this path, and we need to change direction"? What if we recognize, as Einstein pointed out, that we can't solve a problem using the same line of thinking that created the problem in the first place. Let's get specific:

What if we set the tax rates back where they were in the late 1950's when the country was booming?

What if we increased taxes on money earned on money, and reduced taxes on money earned through employment, either ownership of companies that employ people inside the country (dividends for example), or employment earnings because people themselves work. Why should a working person who puts in the effort on the job every day pay 35% in taxes, while someone who just watches the money roll in pays 15%?

What if we tracked down the massive amounts of money that were siphoned from the North American economy though outright fraud and theft, and said, "You have a choice. You can return the money back to the economy and ask for an official pardon for your despicable behavior, or you can go to jail, and we will seize whatever we can get our hands on, no matter where you might have tried to hide it offshore."

What if we tracked down the many cases of sellouts of resources and jobs, and said: "You can put your money back to work in the country, or you can surrender your passport and go live somewhere that needs tapeworms, because you don't represent the values that built this country, and we would frankly be better off as a society and a nation in the long run if you took 'your values' and moved somewhere else, even if you take your money with you. It seems an accident of birth that you are counted as an American or Canadian, when clearly you view yourself as a superior international being with no allegiance to anyone but yourself."

What if even 25% of the wealthiest Americans and Canadians, those who became very well off though hard work, being in the right place at the right time, and having the resources, laws, infrastructure and workforce provided for them, actually renewed their dedication and decided they believed in the countries that are their homeland, in the people that inhabit these lands, and that they want to help bring us back from the brink?

But wait! Where in this North American centric model do we allow for the rest of the world? The answer is pretty simple. We can't help others if we can't help ourselves. We can't show others the path if we have lost our own way.

So we need to all recognize we are on the same spaceship, and need to cooperate and help each other. And not exploit either our brothers in North America, or our brothers in other parts of the world. We can't meet those millennium goals for all mankind until we stabilize and reclaim our own democracy and our own humanity. We can't lead from the back.

What if Corporate Social Responsibility was a fact and a genuine commitment for all companies, not something primarily used as marketing hype and smokescreen. What if Business Social Responsibility groups did not invite tapeworms as guest speakers?

It is a tall order, going from the edge of the abyss back to stability, and then on to peace and harmony, but we have to believe in our hearts that this is possible. We have to dedicate ourselves to this for the sake of our children and our children's children, and we all have to do our part. We need to hold the politicians feet to the fire so that they remember they work for us and for the country – not for multinational corporations intent on getting uber-rich at everyone else's expense.

And it has to be a commitment that **we each individually make** to move us in a positive direction – to take the pledge of Edward Everett Hale:

"I am only one, but I am one. I cannot do everything, but I can do something. And because I cannot do everything, I will not refuse to do the something that I can do. What I can do, I should do. And what I should do, by the grace of God, I will do."

Authors notes, suggested readings, and references:

The journey of writing on a topic of this scope over a relatively short period would have been extremely difficult in an earlier age. We today have the great advantage of high speed Internet, and articles and essays thereon, which in turn hyperlink to other sources; a vast cornucopia of tidbits and treatise on any topic under the sun.

This presents both opportunity and peril, since the scholarly work and the propaganda coexist, with at times seemingly equal weight. During the writing, I endeavored to cross check data across multiple sources, but very specific information can have an error probability. The reader or co-creator is therefore strongly encouraged to perform his or her own investigations on any topic where my data or position seems at variance with your understanding.

With this method of research, comes the corollary that it becomes very difficult to track the exact source of every individual piece of information. I even found places where it was actually forbidden to quote from the source - in that particular case a testimony before a U.S. House committee! I have endeavored to indicate direct sources in line with the text, but since most are web-based publications, there is no guarantee they will still be there if you go looking.

It is interesting to think that in an earlier print-based world, much of the variety and color of reporting was ultimately lost, filtered through the eyes of historians and academics, and often with a particular lens or focal point. The rules change, to an extent, on the web.

Wikipedia articles, for example, may be frequently edited by relatively large numbers of people with specific knowledge and interest in a given subject. I personally consider this process to be more reliable and less prone to any systematic bias than much of what has gone before.

Similarly, I consider local news articles related to specific companies to be generally more reliable than something written by a commentator thousands of miles from the action, and dependent on secondary sources.

So I gravitate towards an article about Nortel in the Ottawa Citizen, for example, rather than in Fox News. And I consider that if a local news article says that businessman X received a jail sentence of fifteen years, this is probably correct, and has not been "fudged" just because it is in the popular press. Truth in advertising - I think it is safe to assume nothing in this narrative came from Fox News or any other highly partisan source of a particular political stripe, except perhaps some of the material from Forbes.com for which I suggested a Cheerleader award.

Some specific recommended sources:

Investopedia.com for relatively clear and factual information on stock market issues, including various bubbles and aberrations throughout history.

Wikipedia.org for many specific details on famous people, such as Adam Smith and Karl Marx, and most of the crooks who have appeared in these pages, like Bernie Ebbers and Jeffrey Skilling.

Bloomsberg.com, Forbes.com for specific information on companies, people, and profits.

Huffingtonpost.ca, Huffingtonpost.com for general news affecting "we the people".

Early in the development of this book, I read **Les Leopold's <u>The Looting of America</u>** from cover to cover. This provided a totally new perspective on the scale and complexity of the problem. Reducing Leopold's place in this narrative to a few paragraphs does not do justice to his influence on my developing understanding, and I would strongly recommend this book, available through Amazon Kindle, among other modes.

Adam Smith's works are largely available as free .pdf although I concentrated on those portions of the <u>Wealth of Nations</u> that dealt with the meaning of money, and the nature of markets and of those who would later be called "capitalists".

I also archived approximately 70 specific Web articles, knowing that such information can be transitory, disappearing into news archives or ending up as dead links. I did provide direct source references where I quoted from specific sources.

Should the reader be unsuccessful in locating some specific information, possibly because it has been archived or removed, I would be happy to oblige a specific request, which can be addressed to me at rabell@rovell.com.

Finding a Team to Work With:

If you have been moved to consider how you might play your part to try to pull us back from the abyss, you will need to align with people and with groups that address some aspect of the problem. Find something that really touches you and dig in. Post, blog, sign petitions, phone and email political, business, and labor leaders. Organize and support campaigns and boycotts.

If you have no idea where to start, you might try a simple Google search on keywords, or you might start with:

en.wikipedia.org/wiki/Activism,
which has links to different types of activism from community building to world peace. You might also want to check:

en.wikipedia.org/wiki/Power_Shift
which has links to organizations involved in the Power Shift movement around the world.

I am aware of a few specific groups that might be of interest, or at least be a starting point. They include U.S., Canadian, and International organizations that are trying to make a difference.

I have listed them alphabetically, as some are focused on a fairly narrow objective, while others are more "cause based". Some are very activist, and some are forums for discussion. A quick visit to any of these web sites should give you a sense of their focus and methods. Find one or more that resonate with you:

Avaaz – www.Avaaz.org
Canadian Parks and Wilderness Society - cpaws.org
Council of Canadians - www.canadians.org
Canadian Department of Peace - www.departmentofpeace.ca
EcoJustice - www.ecojusticc.ca
Fair Vote Canada - www.fairvote.ca
Leadnow - LeadNow.ca
Pachmama Alliance - www.pachamama.org
SME - Take Back Manufacturing - sme-tbm.org
Sum of Us - SumOfUs.org
ThePeaceAlliance - ThePeaceAlliance.org
The Sierra Club - www.sierraclub.org, www.sierraclub.ca

If you identify a serious problem, but do not identify an action-oriented group, why not start one? Nigel Southway and his buddies in the Toronto Chapter of the SME witnessed the demise of manufacturing in Ontario and across North America. Instead of pouring another beer and switching the channel, they started the group to "Take Back Manufacturing". The first meeting in Toronto overfilled the room and ended some time after midnight. Their site is listed above.

Facebook and Linked in, as well as other social media sites also have many group discussions. In fact, as I mentioned at the beginning, it is was discussion in such a group that prompted this book in the first place. So now it is over to you.

About the Author

Dr. Bob Abell is a business owner, a teacher, and an environmentalist. With a Ph.D. in science education, he has a keen interest in the history of science, in ethical science, in health, business, politics, and government.

He is the author of a novel, also published in 2012, called <u>The Corporation</u>.

Made in the USA
Charleston, SC
19 January 2014